J. M. BARRIE
Glamour of Twilight

NEW ASSESSMENTS

J. M. BARRIE

Glamour of Twilight

ALLEN WRIGHT

THE RAMSAY HEAD PRESS EDINBURGH

First Published in 1976 by
The Ramsay Head Press
36 North Castle Street
Edinburgh EH2 3BN

With the support of the
Scottish Arts Council

Printed in Great Britain by
Macdonald Printers (Edinburgh) Limited
Edgefield Road, Loanhead, Midlothian

For
Eleanor, Caroline
Hazel and Angela

Contents

Introduction		11
Chapter One	SUCCESS	17
Chapter Two	"THAT SCOTCH THING"	29
Chapter Three	"A PLAY FOR GROWN UP PEOPLE"	43
Chapter Four	WHAT THE BUTLER SAW	57
Chapter Five	"IT'S NO' NATURAL"	69
Chapter Six	THE HOMECOMING	77
Chapter Seven	"FRAGMENTS OF IMMORTALITY"	89
Appendix		94

I have no such glamour of twilight on my pen.
I am a capable artist; but it begins to look
to me as if you were a man of genius.

Robert Louis Stevenson in a letter to J. M. Barrie

A*

PREFACE

SOME YEARS AGO I had the arrogance to disparage the
work of J. M. Barrie in his favourite theatre—the little
Theatre Royal, Dumfries. Not only was that the first
theatre which he ever entered but it was the place where
he crossed over into the "realms of bliss." On one of
his regular visits there as a schoolboy, the house was
so full that he was invited to stand behind the scenes,
where he fell in love with the idea of play-making.
Nearly 100 years later, Dumfries Guild of Players
presented *Dear Brutus* in that theatre and they asked
me to speak about the play, which I did with what I
now recognise to have been excessive cynicism. The main
target of my scorn was one of the most popular passages
in all of Barrie's writings—the scene in Lob's Wood
between Margaret Dearth and her father. In the estimation of W. A. Darlington, "Nothing that Barrie wrote
for the stage in all his long career was more touching
than this scene." What the former drama critic of the
Daily Telegraph considered to be touching, I found to
be cloying. Such a discrepancy between English and
Socttish evaluations of Barrie's writings was not unusual.

Scots have tended to be more severe, partly out of a
suspicion that Barrie caricatured his fellow-countrymen
for the amusement of foreigners, but mainly because
any exposure of tender feelings is regarded in Scotland
as unmanly, if not mawkish. Some Scottish critics were,
for instance, outraged by the way in which Barrie
exploited his devotion to his mother, revealing in
Margaret Ogilvy intimate details of their relationship.
Long after J. H. Millar had condemned that biography,

George Blake claimed that Barrie very readily sold the pass in all his writings about the Scots. English critics, on the other hand, have considered that Barrie's ability to arouse sympathy was his greatest attribute. James Agate said his "peculiar genius" lay in his knack of bringing out the simple things which were at the back of the spectator's mind.

Of course it would be quite wrong to suggest that he was a prophet without honour in his native land but his work has always been treated with more affection and respect in London than in Kirriemuir. That town's pride in his fame has been tempered by uneasiness about the means by which he achieved it. As well as any lingering resentment which they felt about being presented to the world as the quaint community of Thrums, some people in Kirriemuir kept the Auld Licht burning and disapproved of plays and fiction. While Barrie's birthplace in the Tenements has been preserved as a rather grim museum, the Peter Pan statue in Kensington Gardens is a more fanciful and appropriate monument to his imagination.

Peter Pan may not have been Barrie's finest achievement but it is the work for which he is best known throughout the world, just as *Treasure Island* is probably the most popular of Robert Louis Stevenson's books. The creators of Captain Hook and Long John Silver had much in common. Barrie went to Edinburgh University ten years after Stevenson and greatly regretted that he never met "the king of us all" who, in turn, expressed admiration for his books. The imaginary encounter with R.L.S. which he described in a letter showed that Barrie liked to think they were kindred spirits. Inviting his young compatriot to visit him in

Samoa, Stevenson wrote: "You take the boat to San Francisco and then my place is second to the left"— a sublime simplification of itinerary which surely prompted Peter Pan to give his address as "Second to the right and straight on to morning."

It is curious that Barrie should have been criticised for writing about life in Scotland some thirty years before his time, while Stevenson was never taken to task for delving into the previous century. All the stories Barrie wrote about Thrums were based on his mother's recollections of her childhood, and his skill at recording a vanishing way of life, old customs and forms of speech should be appreciated by anyone who values folk-lore. It has often been suggested that he exaggerated the parsimony and piety of the followers of the Auld Licht, but his mother would have been the first to deplore any distortion of the characters she knew and the way in which they behaved.

In five or six books, only one of which he turned into a play, Barrie milked Thrums dry. Nor was it entirely the milk of human kindness for, despite the reputation he acquired for imparting sweetness and light, his writing was laced with pungent satire. Intolerance, hypocrisy, and an incorrigible weakness for prying into other people's affairs were some of the unpleasant things he observed in Thrums. The books owe much of their vitality, however, to the author's command of Scots vernacular speech. Many of the passages of dialogue are superior to anything in his plays. Apart from the dramatisation of *The Little Minister* and the first act of *What Every Woman Knows*, the plays do not contain much Scots dialogue.

Those who accused him of forsaking Scotland and

writing only for the London stage overlooked the fact that there was no such thing as a Scottish acting profession at the time when Barrie was at the height of his powers as a dramatist. Visiting companies provided most of the drama which was seen in Scotland in those days and any resident companies were predominantly English. There were some accomplished Scots actors working in London but Barrie had to rely on English players to portray most of the Scots characters he created. Their inability to speak with an authentic accent must have troubled him, even if it did not disturb the London critics. John Shand in *What Every Woman Knows* was originally played by Gerald du Maurier and Maggie Wylie by Hilda Trevelyan. The part of Cameron in *Mary Rose* was taken by Ernest Thesiger. Going back to *The Little Minister* in 1897 we find that Cyril Maude was the first Gavin Dishart and nearly all the townsfolk of Thrums were portrayed by Sassunachs. Henders and Pete, the sturdy Scots suitors in *The Professor's Love Story* were first played by Royce Carleton and F. H. Tyler who were out of their element.

In those circumstances, it is not surprising that he wrote few plays which required a mastery of the Scots tongue. *The Boy David* imposed no such strain upon its performers, but it was the only play by Barrie to have its premiere in his native land and, even then, its presentation in Edinburgh was merely a prelude to a London season. It was the last product of a wonderfully fertile mind. Forty years have passed since that play brought his career to an end and so much has been written about the man and his work that yet another act of "Barriolatry" would be superfluous. I did not set out to pay homage, but to inquire into his achievements in

the hope of finding some stuff that will endure. I need
not have feared that I would reach the same conclusion
as the woman who—on seeing the slight figure of
J. M. Barrie robed for his installation as Chancellor
of Edinburgh University—declared: "Och, is he no'
tremendously wee?"

ALLEN WRIGHT

Edinburgh 1976

CHAPTER ONE

SUCCESS

FROM THE ROOF of his flat in Adelphi Terrace, near the Savoy Hotel, J. M. Barrie had a panoramic view extending from the Houses of Parliament to St Paul's Cathedral. It was even more spectacular than usual one night in the autumn of 1917. Searchlights were sweeping the sky where Zeppelins were prowling high above the Thames. To watch this raid on London, Barrie and a group of friends sat on the roof-top. His companions were Thomas Hardy, H. G. Wells, George Bernard Shaw, and Arnold Bennett. In the morning, Barrie found shrapnel strewn around that exposed spot—jagged fragments of shells which, at one fell swoop, could have made English literature much the poorer.

Of course, that illustrious group of writers had, by that time, done most of their best work, but there were still great things to come from some of them. Shaw was writing *Heartbreak House* and Barrie's *Dear Brutus* had just opened in London. Though Barrie was to live for another twenty years, only three more plays of any consequence were to be written by him. These were *Mary Rose, Shall We Join the Ladies?* and *The Boy David*, but he had other contributions to make to the world of literature. His last Scots story, *Farewell Miss Julie Logan* must rank among his finest achievements and the memoirs which he gathered under *The Greenwood Hat* shed much light on his character and on many aspects of his work.

No man who had risen from a humble weaver's cottage to a position of lofty eminence could have failed to marvel at what he had accomplished and, while it would be unfair to say that Barrie gloated over his success, he could not conceal his satisfaction. There is an element of smugness in *The Greenwood Hat* but most of it is written with good-humoured detachment as if the little Scots lad who had made good was not himself, but a figment of his imagination like John Shand or Tommy Sandys. It amused Barrie to think that anyone who looked so insignificant as he did, and who was so lacking in social graces, could have reached the top of London society. As a final touch of conceit, he restricted his memoirs to a limited edition to be privately distributed among his friends—the rich and famous people with whom he was now on a par.

By his diligence and imagination, Barrie had secured privileges beyond the wildest dreams of his youth. If he ever felt that he had swum out of his depth, he kept such thoughts to himself. In conversation, as well as in literary ability, he was probably outshone by most of his companions at that rooftop soiree during an air raid, but they were typical of the company he kept. It gratified him to be on equal terms with the major writers of his day, as well as the statesmen and prominent public figures. The list of guests at a lunch party which Barrie gave in his flat in 1932 provides some indication of his remarkable social status. Among those he entertained on that occasion were Ramsay Macdonald, Stanley Baldwin, the Archbishop of Canterbury, Neville Chamberlain, Sir Austen Chamberlain, John Buchan and Winston Churchill.

Later in the same month, Galsworthy, Chesterton,

18

Wells, and Walter de la Mare were among his guests at Stanway, the mellow mansion in the Cotswolds which Lord Wemyss placed at Barrie's disposal. It was there that he would also entertain visiting celebrities and generally act like an English squire. In his younger days he had gently mocked such lordly figures in some of his plays.

To such an intrepid social climber as Barrie, the supreme conquest must have been his attendance at Princess Margaret's third birthday party at Glamis—the joy being all the greater because this castle was so near his own childhood abode and yet so far above it on the social scale. Barrie's political allegiance was to the Liberals but, at heart, he may have been as much of a Tory as "The Admirable Crichton" for he seemed to share Crichton's conviction that "The most beautiful thing in the world is a haughty aristocratic English house, with everyone kept in his place." Crichton liked to be treated with disdain by his superiors so that he could disdain the lower servants while they, in turn, took it out of "the odds and ends." Barrie was fascinated by a social system which had so many gradations. In Scotland there were really only two classes of people—the educated and the ignorant.

Barrie's infatuation with the life-style of the English upper-class seems to have been based on a mixture of envy, admiration and respect for its languid grace and complete self-assurance. Possibly he resented its exclusiveness and disapproved of its idleness but he was eager to be part of it. Public schools, London clubs, cricket on the village green, pranks on houseboats on the Thames, and weekend parties in country houses; these were some of the things he loved about England

and his interest in them was aroused long before he set foot on that green and pleasant land. Cricket had been his joy "since I first saw it played in infancy by valiant performers in my native parts." The game has flourished in Forfarshire more than in some other parts of Scotland due, it would seem, to the example of a garrison of English troops. Barrie soon found his way to Lord's, when he went to London in 1885 as a young freelance journalist, and there he was thrilled to see the Eton and Harrow match. Many years later he was to have the great satisfaction of watching two of the Llewellyn Davies boys, whom he cherished as if they were his own sons, play for Eton on this sacred turf. He may have mocked the old school tie by making Captain Hook say "Floreat Etona" as he went overboard, but few things in life appeared to give him greater pleasure than steering through Eton the boys who were left in his care. Lady Cynthia Asquith told him he had "a Scotsman's complex about English public schools."

She said he was half beglamoured and half resentful, and could scarcely keep off the subject. In a speech to Wallasey High School of which his niece was head-mistress, he even publicly criticised these schools on the grounds that they were elitist. It was not that he advocated their abolition. He said, "All I am arguing is this, that if they are so splendid, a way in should be found for the boys outside." Though he had no complaints about the education he had received at Dumfries Academy and Edinburgh University, he clearly wished that he had the charm and confidence which was apparently instilled into the scholars at Eton and Harrow, and the students at Oxford and Cambridge. The only thing he had in common with the elegant

English was an ability to play cricket and he formed his own team—the Allahakbarries. Their matches on the village green at Shere were part of the idyllic Victorian scene which entranced Barrie. When the time came for him to act as public benefactor, it is significant that a cricket pavilion was the gift he bestowed on his native town.

Another gentle pastime provided him with material for some stories and for one of his early plays *Walker, London.* This was based on his experiences, larking about on boats around Cookham Lock and the Cliveden Reach of the Thames, where the woodlands sweep down to the water. Jerome K. Jerome may have handled this subject with more success in *Three Men in a Boat* but Barrie's stories in *My Lady Nicotine* are in a similar vein.

That he should, at first, have been so enamoured of London clubs was another sign of his passion for English traditions. He confessed in *The Greenwood Hat* that when he first went to London "clubs were Romance" though he never knew what to do in them. At the age of 29, only four years after his arrival in that city, he was elected a member of the Savage Club. "To think of it," he noted smugly, "and I was once obscure." Frederick Greenwood, the formidable editor of the *St James's Gazette* had nominated him for membership and he had been seconded by one of the great political figures of the time, Lord Rosebery. A year later, when Barrie was on holiday in Scotland, Rosebery invited him to Dalmeny to meet the mighty Gladstone. It is worth noting that he had previously sent Gladstone a copy of *Auld Licht Idylls* for, whatever may be said about Barrie's diffidence and awkwardness, he did not hide his light under a bushel. His rise to prominence would not have been so swift if he had not thrust himself forward.

Of course he was extraordinarily industrious and made a fortune by his pen. He is reputed to have left over £170,000 but when one considers that he earned £80,000 in ten years from the dramatised version of *The Little Minister*, it is obvious that his income from all his work was immense. He went to London confident that he could live on a pound a week and determined to earn a pound a day. By living frugally and working furiously, he laid the foundations of his success. The casual way in which he stuffed cheques into drawers and pockets, and his off-hand attitude to income tax, would suggest, however, that he did not attach much importance to money. He had a greater appetite for fame than for wealth.

It may seem curious that anyone so diligent and ambitious should have wasted time on such leisurely pursuits as cricket, boating and lounging in clubs. The first two of these pastimes were, of course, restricted to the summer months, and his early enthusiasm for clubs soon waned. He was neither idle nor sociable in the first year he spent in Bloomsbury. He was to say, in his Rectorial address at St Andrews University: "The greatest glory that has ever come to me was to be swallowed up in London, not knowing a soul, with no means of subsistence, and the fun of working till the stars went out. To have known anyone would have spoilt it." The man who could talk so fervently about "the fun of working" was like the hero of *The Professor's Love Story* who says: "Ah, work, work, there's nothing like it! The sparkling face of her, when she opens your eyes of a morning and cries, 'Up, up, we have a glorious day's toil before us.' I have run back to her from dinners and marriages and funerals. How often she and I have sat up through the night on tiptoe, so as not to wake the dawn!"

The Professor's trouble was that he was so preoccupied with work that he could not appreciate the fact that he was in love with Lucy, his secretary. Barrie, on the other hand, claimed that he submerged himself in work as a substitute for romance. Writing about Anon, which was the name he gave his younger self, he stated that: "He only strived hard for wealth and fame because he knew he never could impress the ladies." It was not until he became rich and renowned that the ladies were impressed by him. He was well-established as the author of many popular books, even if he was only a novice playwright, when he met Mary Ansell, the actress whom he married.

It is ironical that she almost deprived him of the title which would endorse his fame. Their marriage was approaching its bitter end in the summer of 1909 when he was offered a knighthood. Two other stalwarts of the Stage, Herbert Tree and Arthur Pinero, accepted similar honours at that time but Barrie declined the accolade. The fact that he gladly accepted a baronetcy four years later, when his marriage had been well and truly dissolved, would suggest that he had turned down the first offer simply to prevent Mary Ansell from becoming Lady Barrie. Dennis Mackail, in the authorised biography of Barrie, was being either uncommonly naive or excessively discreet when he brushed all this aside as a simple question of inconsistency. It must have been extremely galling for Barrie to have had to turn down

23

the prize which would have meant so much to him and it is remarkable that he should have dwelt on the subject of honours in two plays which he wrote around that time. In *The Will* which he wrote just before he became a baronet, a lawyer refers to Sir Philip Ross's deceased wife as Lady Ross, thus provoking the self-made man to sharply disclaim her. "She wasn't that" he said, pointing out that his common little wife had died before he had been elevated.

In *The Twelve Pound Look* Barrie ridiculed the pompous vanity of a successful man preparing to receive a knighthood, and the play also dealt with the question of marital incompatibility. It is amazing that such a vulnerable and introspective creature as Barrie should have chosen such delicate topics for the first play to follow his own divorce and disavowal of honours. It was one of Barrie's best works for the stage and, coming only eighteen months after *What Every Woman Knows* it revealed a profound change in the author's attitude to women. While Maggie was content to be her husband's source of inspiration, leaving him to think he had succeeded by his own efforts, the heroine of *The Twelve Pound Look* was as fiercely independent as Nora in Ibsen's *Doll's House*. Not even Bernard Shaw created a more forthright figure of female emancipation than Barrie's spirited Kate who found herself being suffocated by her husband's success and set out to earn her own living. Mary Ansell may have had different reasons for leaving Barrie and probably she bore no resemblance to the character of Kate, but the author's own hunger for success is laughed to scorn in this play.

It is about "that day in your career when everything went wrong just when everything seem to be superlatively right." Harry Sims and his timid wife are rehearsing the ceremony of investiture to which he is looking forward. In his hour of triumph, his first wife turns up in the role of a typist who has been engaged through on agency to answer all the letters congratulating him an his knighthood. Harry believed that Kate had run off with another man many years ago and is horrified to discover that she had no amorous reasons for giving up the life of luxury in which he kept her. She simply could not endure Harry's company any longer and had found that she could support herself by working as a typist. It is not the indignity of her occupation that distresses Harry Sims; it is the thought that anyone could fail to be impressed by his success.

Kate's cynical attitude to the solemn dignity of knighthood would be unusual enough in any play of that period but the fact that the author had just declined such an honour made it all the more startling. Here we have Kate sardonically reeling off all the platitudes about service, duty and reluctance which she is accustomed to putting in the stock letters of reply to congratulatory messages. She even uses the phrase, "Indeed I would have asked to be allowed to decline, had it not been that I want to please my wife"—the exact reversal, it would seem, of Barrie's own situation.

The idea of knighthood being synonymous with success permeates the play and the author could not resist making a jest about the portrait of Harry's second wife having been painted by a knight. In this little comedy, Barrie's satirical skill was seen at his best and his weakness for sentimentality was not at all in evidence. *The Twelve Pound Look* belongs to that small group of sharp plays which modern audiences might find more acceptable than the sweet ones which formed the bulk of his output.

The Will, which was produced in 1913, took a more serious view of human nature being corrupted by success. Though it does not take long to act, its three scenes span thirty years in the life of Philip Ross. He is seen degenerating from a carefree youth with modest ambitions into a prosperous knight who does not know what to do with his fortune. He loves no one. In pursuing material success to the exclusion of all else, he has cut himself off from everyone. *The Will* lacks the twinkling wit of *The Twelve Pound Look* and labours the trite moral that money can not buy happiness but Philip's bewilderment is acutely observed. Success has brought him loneliness and misery. This play was written in the year that Barrie became a baronet and he must have reflected on the bitter irony of gaining an hereditary title when he had no prospect of producing an heir. It is true that he lavished all his affection on the Llewellyn Davies boys and at least some of them reciprocated it, but by this time he was a solitary, sombre figure who must have seen himself shrinking into a rather spiteful imp like Lob in *Dear Brutus* or Sam in *Shall We Join the Ladies?*

In his declining years he developed into an orator, much given to indulging in reminiscences as if to reassure himself that he was once an ordinary person. It was near the end of his term of office as Rector of St Andrews University when he gave his celebrated address on the theme of "Courage." It was a bold choice of subject, considering that many of the students in the audience had been fighting in the trenches four years previously. He soon made it clear to these young men that he was on their side against the Establishment who had allowed the war to happen, and he almost incited them to rebel against their "elders and betters." In possibly the finest passage of that incredibly long speech, he said: "The war has done at least one big thing: it has taken Spring out of the year. And, this accomplished, our leading people are amazed to find that the other seasons are not conducting themselves as usual. The spring of the year lies buried in the fields of France . . ."

On no other public platform did he ever match the theatrical power of the moment when he produced Captain Scott's stained and crumpled letter from the South Pole and read out the words which shimmered with bravery and endurance. Barrie had a marvellous sense of drama.

That address, which lasted about ninety minutes, was extensively reported in the press and all his subsequent speeches were recorded in *The Times* as if he were an elder statesman. He enjoyed greater prestige than any other writer. Honorary degrees were conferred on him and he received the Order of Merit. To his great delight, he became Chancellor of his alma mater and few things seem to have given him more pleasure than having the gift of patronage—the right to nominate other distinguished people for honorary degrees. As Rector of St Andrews, his list of laureates included Thomas Hardy, Sidney Colvin, John Galsworthy, E. V. Lucas and Ellen Terry. As Chancellor of Edinburgh University he chose to confer degrees on Harley Granville-Barker, Neil Munro and Sir Arthur Quiller-Couch. At lunch in the students' union, after his installation, he even boasted of all the Prime Ministers he had known.

Only one of them, Ramsay Macdonald, was in the

27

procession of mourners that followed Barrie to his last resting place at Kirriemuir seven years later. Also present on that occasion was Sir Harry Lauder, the only other Scotsman to receive a title for his stagecraft. Lauder and Barrie, in their different ways, gave the world a weird impression of Scotland, but both of them had tenacity as well as talent. Lauder's exhortation to keep right on to the end of the road was not wasted on Barrie who once said that his only asset was "a certain grimness about not being beaten."

CHAPTER TWO

"THAT SCOTCH THING"

WHEN J. M. BARRIE's father descended on London, the first place he wanted to see was Thomas Carlyle's house in Cheyne Row, Chelsea. Like so many Scottish families in the Victorian era, the Barries had an even higher regard for Carlyle than for Burns. The sage of Ecclefechan was, on Barrie's admission, "the only writer I ever tried to imitate."

Carlyle died in 1881, three years after Barrie had left Dumfries Academy for Edinburgh University. In *The Greenwood Hat*, Barrie recalled that during his schooldays at Dumfries, "I often saw Carlyle in cloak, sombrero and staff, mooning along our country roads, a tortured mind painfully alone, even to the eyes of a boy." Young Barrie always doffed his cap to him. "I daresay I paid this homage fifty times, but never was there any response." If he did not receive as much as a nod of recognition from the venerable Carlyle, he was certainly to win the admiration of another great Scots man of letters, Robert Louis Stevenson. From distant Samoa he wrote many encouraging words to Barrie but it was in a letter to Henry James in 1892 that Stevenson made his shrewdest observations: "Barrie is a beauty, *The Little Minister* and *The Window in Thrums* eh? Stuff in that young man; but he must see and not to be too funny. Genius in him, but there's a journalist at his elbow—there's the risk."

It was through journalism that Barrie learned his craft and his first books were simply collections of articles which he wrote for various papers—principally the *St James's Gazette* and the *British Weekly*. His career in journalism began while he was still a student, writing book reviews for *The Scotsman* and dramatic criticism for the *Edinburgh Courant*. Apart from a brief engagement as a leader writer on the *Nottingham Journal* he was a free-lance all his days. In *Barrie: The Story of a Genius* Sir John Hammerton said that it was fortunate the aspiring author joined the staff of a "third-rate" provincial newspaper. "It would have been a misfortune for our young journalist had he been appointed to the editorial staff of *The Scotsman* (which was naturally his immediate ambition) or the *Glasgow Herald*. These papers were prosperous enough to employ large staffs of adequately paid writers and sub-editors, and the inclination to settle down obscurely but comfortably as a 'member of the staff' was a snare which ambitious youth had to guard against."

Barrie had the journalist's knack of being able to judge which subjects would interest a wide range of readers and, at first, it did not occur to him that there would be a market in London for the quaint stories his mother had told him about her childhood in Kirriemuir. He did, however, include one in a batch of articles which he sent to Frederick Greenwood, editor of the *St James's Gazette* who rejected most of them but scribbled a note saying "I liked that Scotch thing. Any more of those?"

On November 17, 1884, it was printed unsigned, under the title "An Auld Licht Community." At the age of 24, Barrie was on the road to success and "Auld Licht" funerals, courtships, scandals and weddings flowed from his pen. These sketches, along with some that had not previously appeared in the press, were gathered together in one volume, *Auld Licht Idylls*. The critics received the book with enthusiasm verging on rapture. The *Academy* hailed it as "not only the best book dealing exclusively with Scotch humble life, but the only book of the kind deserving to be classed as literature that has been published for at least quarter of a century." This is a point of some significance, for it shows that Barrie was a late-comer to the Kailyard and not, as some critics have suggested, its instigator. Even his admirers have conceded that a swarm of trumpery Scots stories, reeking of sentimentality, *followed* the publication of *Auld Licht Idylls* and *A Window in Thrums*. Roger Lancelyn Green in his introduction to a collection of Barrie's plays and stories (published by Dent in 1962) stated that: "The immense popularity of these brilliant pictures of a bygone Kirriemuir, based on his mother's recollections of her girlhood, brought a nemesis upon Barrie in the shape of a host of inferior imitators, the calculating sentimentalists of the 'Kailyard' school, headed by S. R. Crockett and 'Ian Maclaren.' Barrie's distinctive originality and selective realism came beneath the sickly shadow of *The Lilac Sunbonnet* and have long lain neglected 'Beside the Bonnie Briar Brush'."

Of course Barrie had imitators but it is important to note that he was not the first to till the Kailyard. He simply did it better than anyone else. Roger Lancelyn Green's "nemesis" is difficult to reconcile with this passage from the *Spectator* review of *Auld Licht Idylls*: "In its fidelity to truth, its humour and its vivid interest, it is a complete and welcome contrast to the paltry 'duds' which are nowadays printed by the dozen as pictures of humble and religious life in Scotland." It was those paltry "duds" which flourished in the Kailyard. The best of Barrie's sketches and stories do not belong there and his reputation has greatly suffered from being associated with a worthless literary movement. It is possible that his mention of kail on the first page of *Auld Licht Idylls* was intended as a joke but it certainly rebounded on him. "The Kail," says the narrator, "grows brittle from the snow in my dank and cheerless garden."

J. H. Millar, one of the most influential Scottish critics of the time, may be held chiefly responsible for dumping Barrie in the Kailyard. In the *New Review* in 1895, Millar wrote: "It is a fact that J. M. Barrie is fairly entitled to look upon himself as Pars Magna if not Pars Maxima of the great Kailyard movement." He repeated that back-handed compliment in his *History of Scottish Literature* (1902).

About fifty years later, George Blake compounded this error in a book called *Barrie and the Kailyard School*. It tells us more about the latter than about Barrie, though Blake seems to have been anxious to emphasise that Barrie was a better dramatist than novelist. Referring to *The Little Minister*, Blake remarks that "It will always be a puzzle that one of the most expert craftsmen the theatre has ever known was so ham-fisted over the long, slow stretches of fiction." In Barrie's own estimation, on the other hand, the dramatised version of *The Little Minister* was unworthy of the original novel and he once said that he intended to omit it from any further collections of his plays which might be published.

Blake was critical, not only of Barrie's prose style, but of his attitude to his ain folk. In Blake's view, he very readily sold the pass: "One thinks to perceive in Barrie's Kailyard writings either a positive dislike of his own people or a blatant desire to gratify the prejudices of other people." That is probably the most serious charge that has been laid against him. Even such an ardent admirer as Roger Lancelyn Green detected a "cynical" note in *Auld Licht Idylls* and *A Window in Thrums* but said it was not to be found in *The Little Minister*. Green admitted that Barrie may have set out to caricature the society of Kirriemuir but he was soon converted "by the sterling worth and the basic nobility of these simple followers of the Old Light." That may seem to be pitching it at the other extreme from Blake. The truth lay somewhere between these assessments. It was with affectionate amusement that Barrie studied the denizens of Thrums. He could appear to be patronising but was more often penetrating in his observation. *Auld Licht Idylls* and *A Window in Thrums* are examples of a curious hybrid—sympathetic satire.

The names which he gave the places and the characters, like Glen Quharity and the McQumpha family, cheapened the stories, for they would seem to have been designed to puzzle and amuse English readers. Anyone called Hendry McQumpha was liable to be taken as a caricature, but the mockery went no further than that. The only people to whom Barrie extended no mercy were the "unco guid." Scotland is still full of men like Bowie Haggart who told a meeting of Thrums Literary Society: "I am of the opeenion that the work of Burns is of an immoral tendency. I have not read them myself, but such is my opeenion." Tammas Haggart's solemn dissertation on his sense of humour is another example of earnest folly. "A Humorist" says Tammas, "would often no ken 'at he was ane if it wasna by the wy he maks other fowk lauch."

While most of the pathos of these books now tastes like syrup, the humorous passages are as sharp as ever. There is a delightful chapter in *A Window in Thrums* entitled "Preparing to Receive Company." Jess issues a stream of instructions to the family about how they should behave when their genteel visitor arrives.

"Dinna stir yer tea as if ye was churnin' butter" she says, "nor let on 'at the scones is no our ain bakin'." In another warning to them all to be on their best behaviour, she says, "If Tibbie says onything aboot the china, yer no' to say 'at we dinna use it ilka day." This was not the only chapter in which Barrie made it clear that a passion for keeping up appearances was the chief concern of Thrums folk. Pride and piety went hand in hand—an unholy alliance summed up in a phrase spoken by old Nany Wabster in *The Little Minister*: "The most blessed thing I can think of is to be sitting reverent in the kirk, and to be in the fashion at the same time."

By undoing all their efforts to keep up appearances, Barrie did not endear himself to the people of Kirriemuir. One could argue that it was their hypocrisy which he debunked and that he did not scoff at their simple faith or frugal way of life. Barrie would never have deliberately derided family life. He could see its frailties and its comical aspect but he always acknowledged the debt which Scottish literature owed to the closeness of the Scots family. The domestic hearth, he said, had been its chief source of inspiration since long before the days of Burns. In the first act of *What Every Woman Knows* he paid his supreme tribute to the Scottish family.

There he showed that fathers and brothers might pretend to exercise authority but the real power resided in women. All the Thrums stories exploded the myth that Victorian Scotland was a patriarchal society. Hendry McQumpha may be an imposing figure but he is subservient to Jess. In *Sentimental Tommy*, the father is conspicuous by his absence. His widow does not mourn the fact that he has died but that she ever married him. Dying was the only kindness he ever did her. In *Margaret Ogilvy*, poor David Barrie is scarcely mentioned. Of course J. M. Barrie's mother fixation was of monumental proportions, and it was from her that he acquired his command of the Scots tongue. "We always spoke to each other in broad Scotch" he said, adding (at the age of 70), "I think in it still."

His liberal use of Scots words and phrases evidently did not deter English and American readers. No glossaries were provided, but in his early books, the English equivalents of some words were printed in parentheses. To "keek," for example, was interpreted as "to glance," and "curran" as "number of" but many words were left untranslated even though their meaning can not have been clear to anyone unfamiliar with vernacular Scots. The use of "greeting" in the sense of "crying" may have baffled some people. Occasionally he would use a spate of Scots phrases for comic effect, as in the dramatised version of *The Little Minister* when Lord Rintoul and Captain Halliwell are at a loss to understand the villagers' descriptions of the girl who has vanished into the woods:

" 'She's snod but no unco snod'

'I mean she's a couthie tawpie but no sair in order'

'A tasty stocky but no happit up to the nines'
'She was a ga'en about hizzie an' giy an' custie'
'A well-faured custie, perjink and fell orra'."

In that passage he was deliberately using archaic
words to form an impenetrable Scotch mist. Fortunately,
he rarely indulged in such exhibitions and he valued the
vituperative power of the Scots tongue more highly
than its picturesque aspect. Jean Myles, the mother of
Sentimental Tommy, wrote the most scathing letters in
the vernacular. Reduced to poverty in London, her
only pleasure was boasting to the folk at home in Thrums
that she was living in grand style. To the hated Esther
Auld she would write: "And ony bonny afternoon
when your man is cleaning out stables and you're at the
tub in a short gown, picture my man taking me and the
children out a ride in a carriage, and I sair doubt your
bairns was never in nothing more genteel than a coal
cart. For bairns is yours, Esther, and children is mine,
and that's a burn without a brig till't."

The tragic figure of Jean Myles, the victim of "a
magerful man," may be a minor character study but
Barrie's account of her downfall is one of the best
passages of narrative which he wrote. The opening
chapters of *Sentimental Tommy*, depicting life in a poor
quarter of London where the exiles from Thrums have
settled, have a Dickensian flavour. Tommy and his fellow
urchins have much more vitality than Wendy and her
brothers in *Peter Pan* but that, of course, only underlines
the difference between bairns and children.

His books are predominantly Scottish but the plays
(with the exception of *The Little Minister* which origin-
ated in the form of a novel) have little connection with

Scotland. It is the setting of two acts of *The Professor's Love Story*, the first two acts of *What Every Woman Knows* and the second act of *Mary Rose*. In each case it is seen from afar as a place to go for holidays or as a country from which bright young men must escape to seek fame and fortune in London. Unlike Stevenson, whose work became more Scottish the longer he spent in exile, Barrie appeared to lose interest in Scotland as a source of literary inspiration. It was almost as if he wished to sever his connections with anywhere so primitive as Thrums, and show that he was more at ease in sophisticated English society.

Then, at the age of seventy-one, when he had apparently finished with writing, he composed the finest Scottish story of them all. It belongs to that great band of the supernatural, which marches through Scots literature, led by *Tam o' Shanter* and Stevenson's *Thrawn Janet*.

Farewell Miss Julie Logan was published as a supplement to *The Times* on Christmas Eve 1931 and between hard covers the following year. In it Barrie returned to the neighbourhood of Thrums—to a place not unlike Glen Quharity and to a character bearing a close resemblance to the Rev. Gavin Dishart, "The Little Minister." The period was about thirty years later than that of the Thrums stories; the narrative style much more assured and refined. It takes the form of a diary, with an epilogue written a quarter of a century afterwards. Like Dishart, the Rev. Adam Yestreen is a prim young Presbyterian who is enraptured by a girl of infinite charm. While Babbie was simply unreal, Julie Logan is genuinely ethereal. Both characters would seem to represent the romantic ideal which eluded Barrie.

Adam Yestreen is keeping the diary for the benefit of the English who come to the "Grand House" in August, for the grouse-shooting. They have challenged him to record what happens in the winter when the glen is cut off by snow for weeks or months. It is then that the "strangers" are supposed to appear and Adam, who is new to the parish, has been told that, "You 'go queer' yourself without knowing it, and walk and talk with these doolies, thinking they are of your world till maybe they have mischieved you." Adam regards such tales as "superstitious havers" but he has enough Highland blood in him to be intrigued by the possibility of spirits haunting the glen. He preaches in Gaelic once every Sunday, as enjoined, to the few "pure Heilandmen" who remain in these parts. He also has what he considers to be a weakness for the fiddle, which interfered with his studies at St Andrews University. He has never played it since being called to the ministry though he occasionally takes it out of its case to fondle the strings.

Barrie skilfully and discreetly drops all these clues to Adam's character, to show that this is no dull, orthodox Lowland preacher who might be impervious to the supernatural. Adam may be strait-laced but he has a hankering for romance and beauty. Even the way he describes his surroundings reveals that he is no ordinary Presbyterian. "Round the manse" he says, "there are grossart-bushes, rizers and rasps, a gean, bee-skeps and the like, that in former hands were called the yard, but I call it the garden." His narrative is couched in self-consciously correct English, as if Adam was acutely aware of being an educated Scotsman, but evocative Scots words and phrases creep into it instinctively and sometimes deliberately, because he likes the sound of them.

He refers, for example, to the jargonelle tree being "in flourish," pointing out that the English would say in blossom—"a word with no gallantry intilt." This is not simply a case of Barrie being nostalgic and airing his recollections of his mother-tongue. It is all part of the subtle process of establishing that Adam has a poetic heart ruled by a puritanical head. Julie Logan is conjured up by his romantic nature and rejected by his bigoted conscience.

There is much of Barrie's own character in Adam Yestreen—not least his attitude towards the English gentry. He is conscious of being quaint and awkward in their company and yet is eager to be accepted by them on equal terms. In a revealing passage, Adam recalls a visit to the Grand House where the English were very hospitable to him, "giving me the most attractive lady to take in on my arm to dinner, and putting the most popular man on the other side of her to make up for me. They are so well-meaning that it would have vexed them to know I noticed this." That is a clear example of Barrie writing from experience, his sense of inferiority being counter-balanced by the satisfaction of seeing through their conduct. He could also chuckle at their affectations of Scottishness, as when he says "The bright array of their kilts is a pretty bit colour to us, the trousered people of the glen" or when he notes that they use the word "clachan" to describe what the local people know as "the five houses."

The story reaches its climax on Hogmanay—"always a night of solemn gallanting." In several of his books, Barrie referred to the ancient traditions of those revels.

39

He went into this subject in some detail in *Sentimental Tommy*, and *Auld Licht Idylls* contains the most perfect description of their aftermath: "The Daft Days—the black week of glum debauchery that ushers in the year." Barrie's work might well be more popular today if he had elaborated upon that glum debauchery but that was not his inclination. The "gallanting" of Hogmanay and its supernatural associations were more to his liking than the sensual excesses of the New Year festivities. Similarly, while it was all right for Julie Logan to be wayward, it would never have done for her to be wanton. Adam Yestreen's aberrations were spiritual rather than carnal.

Of the landscape in which this story is set, there is scant description. The Thrums stories are equally bereft of scenery. Woodlands and glens are matters of fact and not things of beauty. It would seem that, in addition to all her other powerful influences on his life, Margaret Ogilvy was to blame for Barrie's lack of interest in the landscape. "My mother did not care for scenery" he said, "and that is why there is so little of it in my books."

Without describing the terrain of Adam Yestreen's parish, Barrie succeeded in establishing an atmosphere of remoteness and desolation. The young minister's picturesque turn of phrase often dispels the gloom, however. Referring to a fiddler playing outside a cottage, he says, "It is pretty to hear him in the gloaming, letting the songs loose like pigeons." Instead of making the prosaic observation that his parishioners live in humble dwellings, he notes that the study and dining-room of the manse are the only two rooms in the glen "without a bed in them."

The story has a richer texture than any of Barrie's earlier books and it makes one wonder if he was wise to abandon writing novels and essays and devote the greater part of his career to the stage. He said himself, in *The Greenwood Hat*: "I preferred writing books and still think they were more my game." He was never sure whether A. B. Walkley, William Archer and George Meredith had done him a great disservice by encouraging him to write plays. Walkley began by deploring his attempts at play-writing which he considered to be much inferior to the books, but changed his mind when he saw *The Admirable Crichton*. From then on, with all the zeal of a convert, he could find no fault in Barrie's plays. Even J. A. Hammerton had to admit that he had been short-sighted. In 1900 Hammerton produced a series of critical essays under the heading of *J. M. Barrie and his Books* in which he wrote: "As an old student of the acted drama, I have no compunction in expressing the opinion that, despite the wonderful success of *The Little Minister* on the stage, Mr Barrie is not, and is never likely to be, a serious factor in the contemporary drama. . . . His genius can best be shaped in books and not in plays."

At the turn of the century, no one expected that Thrums would be eclipsed by a galaxy of plays.

CHAPTER THREE

"A PLAY FOR GROWN UP PEOPLE"

BARRIE CLAIMED THAT he never had any ambitions to
become a playwright. The theatre and the oddities of
its life attracted him but plays did not. He was fascinated
by the whole "clamjamfry" of actors, call-boys, stage-
door keepers, and dressers—the only uninteresting
figure being the playwright. In his schooldays at Dumfries, he delighted to watch the old actor-managers and
their companies of vagabonds presenting colourful
fragments of Shakespeare's tragedies, punctuated by
song and dance, with the performance culminating in a
farce. As a student in Edinburgh, he would wait at pit
doors to be "haunted by the dire orbs of Irving." He
liked to sit at the end of the front row so that he could
see what was happening in the wings. The process of
make-believe intrigued him more than the result. He
said, at the age of seventy, that "I am like that still, in
the sense that though I suppose I don't go to a play
nowadays twice in the year, I should still be happy and
interested in looking on at the rehearsal of anything."

Barrie would much rather sit alone in an empty
theatre, watching the preparations, than be surrounded
by an audience at a performance. For one who professed to have so little interest in plays, he was surprisingly
anxious to ensure that the actors adhered closely to the
script and to the original directions he gave them. He
did not acquire the reputation of being a master-
craftsman without an effort and it is hard to believe

his assertion that he never gave stage-craft any conscious thought. Harley Granville-Barker who knew Barrie well, and was also well-versed in the techniques of playwriting, saw through that pretence. He noted that "Barrie was already an accomplished writer of essays and novels when he first gave his mind at all seriously to the theatre. Having done so, he set to work painstakingly to learn its craft, not presuming in the least upon the earlier achievement."

Such was his skill at writing dialogue, however, that he was already half-way to becoming a playwright. Some passages from his books would lend themselves, without any adjustment, to performance on the stage. Barrie himself said that his fondness for writing in dialogue was what lured him on to write plays. He even wrote letters in dialogue, and said he would preach in it if he were a clergyman, and write his prescriptions in it if he were a physician. It seemed to come so naturally to him that the reader has no difficulty in following the text of the plays. Barrie need not have added the linking narrative to the "library" editions. His dialogue is almost invariably superior to the embellishments—those knowing comments which he added to the plays long after they had been performed.

Tastes have changed since A. E. Wilson wrote, in a foreword to the collected plays, that it was a pity the first four plays lacked introductions "and that linking together of the scenes, those explanations of the motives and emotions of his characters, which give such added charm and narrative interest in the reading of his later plays." The explanations were superfluous and there is more whimsy to be found in these afterthoughts than in any of the acting texts. Possibly the best service

44

which anyone could render to Barrie would be to publish a volume of his best plays, shorn of all the interpolations. Some examples must be quoted. When John Shand is elected to Parliament in the second act of *What Every Woman Knows*, Maggie Wylie's father and brothers hoist her on to their shoulders. "The queer little elated figure is raised aloft" notes Barrie, preciously adding, "With her fingers, she can just touch the stars." Later in the same play he is not content to say "Exit Lady Sybil" but "She passes into the dining-room looking as pretty as a kiss." The last scene of *The Admirable Crichton* is ruined by the ponderous witticisms which Barrie put in parentheses. Crichton, we are gratuitously told, is "an enigma to the last" and when Lady Mary asks if he despises her, the author interjects: "The man who could never tell a lie makes no answer."

Dear Brutus is drenched in inconsequential comments. We are told that Margaret Dearth "has as many freckles as there are stars in heaven. She is as lovely as you think she is, and she is aged the moment when you like your daughter best." Barrie's weakness for investing inanimate objects or places with human feelings manifested itself often enough in the dialogue, but even more in these elaborate trimmings. In the published text of *Mary Rose*, for instance, he observes that "There are rooms that are always smiling, so that you may see them at it if you peep through the keyhole."

Having turned one book into a play, he proceeded to reverse the process so that the plays would give as much pleasure to the reader in his armchair as to the spectator in the stalls. Cynics might say that he wanted the best of both worlds—the profit to be had from the stage, and the esteem of the much wider public that could be reached through the printed page. In the long run, however, the merit of some of the plays has been obscured by the frills he attached to them. In this respect, he was the opposite of George Bernard Shaw whose prefaces were often better than his plays.

Considering that the careers of Barrie and Shaw ran in parallel for forty years it is surprising that there have not been more comparative studies of their work. Allardyce Nicoll (in *English Drama 1900-1930*) suggested that both men were essentially sentimental: "Shaw's was the sentimentality of the mind, Barrie's of the heart." Dr Nicoll said that "Barrie had wisdom but not the mental force by which wisdom attains power. Barrie had no new ideas to express; Shaw so habitually dwelt in the world of ideas and concepts that often human beings became lost amid the notions."

A revival of *What Every Woman Knows* at Pitlochry Festival Theatre in 1976 prompted a modern playwright, Tom Gallacher, to make the astonishing statement that "Shaw's plays died before he did and are unlikely to be revived." Gallacher went on to claim that Barrie's work had more enduring qualities. Shaw, he said, was not just out of favour—"He is out of the running because, quite simply, he lacked 'heart.' Less sentimentally he lacked that direct use of personal emotion and feeling which Barrie could rarely avoid." He added that "Shaw used his astonishing talent on things that were outside him. Barrie, increasingly, used only what was within. There have been many writers who had more "within" than J. M. Barrie but few who used their resources with such full and childlike honesty."

Shaw was not as contemptuous of Barrie's work as one might have expected the champion of "The New

Drama" to be. Writing to Johnston Forbes Robertson in 1903, when *Quality Street* and *The Admirable Crichton* were in full swing, Shaw said, "I have actually taken to going to the theatre to see Barrie's plays; and I not only stand them without discomfort, but enjoy them."

The two playwrights became good friends, working together for many causes—not least the crusade against theatre censorship. Apart from *The Wedding Guest* which ran for 100 performances in 1900, Barrie wrote nothing which was likely to incur the Lord Chamberlain's displeasure, but he was acutely conscious of his responsibilities as one of the leading dramatists in Britain. Both Shaw and Barrie contributed to the Frohman repertory season at the Duke of York's Theatre in 1910 when Shaw's *Misalliance* had fewer performances than *The Twelve Pound Look* by Barrie. During that season, Shaw wrote to August Strindberg whose work he hoped to introduce to London and, in this context, it may seem extraordinary that he used *Peter Pan* as an example.

Shaw was trying to convince Strindberg that a production in London of his *Lucky Peter's Travels* might pave the way for sterner stuff like *Miss Julie*. In the course of Shaw's long letter to Strindberg, it is stated that: "A few years ago, one of our most popular authors, J. M. Barrie, wrote a sort of fairy play for children called *Peter Pan* which had such an enormous success that it has since been revived every Christmas, ostensibly as a holiday entertainment for children, but really as a play for grown-up people; for, as you know, when we buy toys for children, we take care to select the ones which amuse ourselves. Ever since this happened it has been the dream of every London manager to find another Peter Pan. . . ."

Managers continue to have that dream, and *Peter Pan* crows every year. In the last century of British Theatre, the operas of Gilbert and Sullivan are the only other works to have enjoyed such uninterrupted popularity. No one would claim that *Peter Pan* or the Savoy Operas were great works of art but they can still cast a spell over audiences. Captain Hook, who is one of Barrie's most colourful creations, is very much a Gilbertian figure. His oaths and exclamations are richly ridiculous —as when he says, "Obesity and bunions, 'tis a princely scheme" or "By Caius and Balbus"—and his hearty dislike of children serves as an antidote to the sickly sweet stuff in the play. Before he goes to his doom, does he not declare that there is something grand in the idea of a holocaust of children? Anthony Hope was simply echoing Hook's sentiments when he yearned for "an hour of Herod" after seeing *Peter Pan.*

Most people are not so disturbed by the play's over-indulgent attitude to children as they are by its fulsome obsession with mothers. It is surprising that today's young audiences do not jeer at the Lost Boys when they cry in unison: "What we need is just a nice motherly person" and Wendy replies, "Oh dear, I feel that is just exactly what I am." Even Hook suffers from a mother-fixation and wants to make Wendy the mother of his pirate crew. The relationship between Peter and Wendy is very peculiar. She treats him as the father of the Lost Boys, from which it follows that he should act as her husband, but Peter will have none of it. "I just always want to be a little boy and have fun" he says and when Wendy asks him "What are you to me?" he infuriates her by saying, "Your son, Wendy." The play contains so much of this kind of thing that it would seem to be as bad as giving children rich damp cake. The strange Freudian under-currents of *Peter Pan* certainly do not account for its continuing popularity. It survives, in spite of them, because its surface attractions are so great and its imaginative qualities are so delicate.

Peter's entrance through the nursery window is a wonderfully theatrical stroke that has few equals (unless one counts John Shand's first appearance in *What Every Woman Knows*). The magic of Peter's arrival is compounded by having Tinker Bell appear simultaneously and plonk herself into a jug. What makes the advent of these other-worldly creatures all the more marvellous is that they are looking for something as insubstantial as a shadow. The one good deed which Wendy renders Peter is to sew on that shadow. She spends the rest of the play trying to subdue and smother his wild spirit.

In many parts of the world, *Peter Pan* is the only work for which Barrie is renowned. Even in his native land, there are countless people to whom the name of Barrie means nothing else but *Peter Pan*. On grounds of popularity (and because it touches heights of fantasy) it must take pride of place in any list of his writings. Since his death in 1937, not many of his other plays have been performed in London. The only ones to have been revived with any frequency in Scotland have been *The Admirable Crichton*, *Dear Brutus* and *What Every Woman Knows*. There have been a few productions of *Mary Rose* and one notable revival of *The Twelve Pound Look* (at Pitlochry Festival Theatre in 1966). No one now dares to resurrect his last play *The Boy David* which, after its premiere in Edinburgh, had only 55 performances in London. His first play to enjoy any success, *Ibsen's*

49

Ghost, has been neglected for even longer and has not had a professional production since J. L. Toole presented it in 1891.

In the spring of that year *Hedda Gabler*, *Ghosts* and *Rosmersholm* were performed in London for the first time and *A Doll's House* was seen again. The Ibsen controversy was at its height. As well as being reviled by the majority of critics, the plays were the subject of great dispute between the translators, William Archer and Edmund Gosse. Shaw joined in the fray and published his enthusiastic "Quintessence of Ibsenism" while Clement Scott led the opposition whose prim sense of decency was outraged. *Ghosts* was condemned as a foul and filthy concoction, a loathesome sore unbandaged, a dirty act done publicly. Passions were running high when Barrie's burlesque arrived upon the scene.

It shows such a grasp of Ibsen's style that it is much more than a frivolous skit. Realising afterwards that it had been the height of impudence to parody the greatest dramatist of his age, Barrie refrained from publishing the text of *Ibsen's Ghost*. It did not appear in public print until 1975 when Penelope Griffin presented two versions of the text with an extensive commentary. From reading them it is apparent that Barrie had a much deeper appreciation of Ibsen's work than any of the critics who became so agitated about it. *Ibsen's Ghost* is a brilliant piece of satire which would give much pleasure if it were to be performed today.

The scene is set in George Tesman's House, as in *Hedda Gabler*. Following the suicide of that lady, George has married Thea Elvsted whom he absent-mindedly addresses as "darling Hedda." She is planning

50

to desert him, just like her last husband, but George is too preoccupied with his books to notice her loss of affection for him. "Do you know" he says naively, "Judge Brack told me yesterday he envied me my pretty little wife. Just think of that." When Thea rapturously reveals that Judge Brack kissed her, the fatuous scholar seems quite unconcerned. Thea's grandpapa, who seems like a caricature of Ibsen, enters the room to find her standing over the stove burning the 127 love letters which George wrote to her. The old man is shocked to learn that she is leaving her husband and that she has allowed herself to be kissed not only by Judge Brack but also by Parson Greig, Henrik Borsam and Baron Kleig! Grandpapa is stricken with remorse and staggers around, muttering about "ghosts." He must tell the secret that has been burdening his conscience for forty years. "It is I who have made you what you are" he says, launching into an emotional tirade about hereditary weakness. In all the time that he has been married to Thea's grandmother he has never had a moment's happiness because of the dreadful thing he did on the eve of their wedding. He kissed one of her bridesmaids. The impulse was so strong that he could not resist it.

Thea recovers from the shock of learning that her propensity for kissing can be put down to heredity. "Grandpapa," she says, "your confession has made a woman of me. It has turned me into a Hedda." A new era is dawning when old conditions will be played out and new conditions will take their place, banishing for ever such things as heredity and grandfathers. At this juncture, the old man's wife enters and begins to behave like Nora in *A Doll's House*. She accuses him of not allowing her to lead her own life. He had even stood

51

by and allowed her children to call her mother—the ultimate indignity for a woman. He is denounced as "a disgracefully healthy old man" and is offered Hedda Gabler's pistol so that he can leave this contemptible world. The ladies having been persuaded to make an equally noble exit, they all die, and George returns to observe casually, "Someone been shooting rubbish here? Just fancy that."

Even Archer, the leader of the "Ibsenites" was amused by Barrie's burlesque which, if it did nothing else, punctured the pomposity displayed by the opposing factions in the Ibsen controversy. What made it even funnier was the fact that "Grandpapa" was played by the most amiable and old-fashioned of comic actors, J. L. Toole. It was as aptly irreverent as *Waiting for Godot* might be, if the tramps were portrayed by Morecambe and Wise.

Barrie pounced on Ibsen's habit of repeating certain phrases like "Just think of that" or "Fancy that" which Dr Griffin informs us are spoken by Tesman no less than thirty-five times in *Hedda Gabler*. It was not only the outward appearance of Ibsen's plays which Barrie parodied. On occasions, the satire went deeper as when George looks up from a manuscript to inquire "Is there a 'K' in Christianity?" and Thea replies, "There is nothing in Christianity."

In the same year that *Ibsen's Ghost* was presented at Toole's Theatre, there were performances in London of Barrie's one act play *Becky Sharp* and of *Richard Savage* which he wrote in collaboration with R. B. Marriott Watson. He had no success with either of these, and his next attempt at working in partnership with another writer was an equally dismal failure. That was the

operetta *Jane Annie* on which his collaborator was
Arthur Conan Doyle.

Walker, London was the first full-length play by
Barrie to be profitable, and it ran for over 500 performances. This trivial story of an impostor who amuses
smart young people on a houseboat would not hold the
stage now but it retains its place in the Barrie saga
because it was through this play that he met Mary
Ansell. She took one of the leading roles in the first
production and married the author two years after that
comedy opened at Toole's Theatre. In his next play,
The Professor's Love Story, and in the dramatised version
of *The Little Minister*, Barrie had much to say about the
process of falling in love and always made it appear to
be a trap into which men were lured against their will.
As Snecky puts it, at the end of *The Little Minister*:
"It has come to this, as it comes to every son of Adam.
For a while he thinks women is the poor miserable
criturs we all ken them to be, till on a woeful day he
sees one, very like the others, and something inside him
goes crack, whether he be highly edicated or highly
ignorant." Cosens, the London doctor in *The Professor's
Love Story* is rather more subtle but equally defeatist
when he says: "My dear Tom, when women love us we
should never ask why. All we can be sure of is that they
see something in us which isn't there."

By the turn of the century, Barrie's attitude to love
had become less pawky. In *The Wedding Guest* which
was produced in 1900 (and in *Tommy and Grizel* which
was published about the same time) he observed the
bitter tensions between men and women. Writing in a
more jocular vein some years later, he noted that "Real
plays are always about a lady and two men; and, alas,

only one of them is her husband. That is Life, you know."

The Wedding Guest was one of the few attempts he made, as a dramatist, to come to grips with "Life." Realism was never to be his forte. "I know of no other writer" said James Agate, "who has burked life so exquisitely." It is possible that Barrie was determined to shake off the reputation of being an escapist and wrote *The Wedding Guest* to show that he could face facts. That is exactly what Mr Fairbairn, one of the characters in the play, is incapable of doing. He flinches from reality but deludes himself that he is an optimist, always looking on the bright side of things. When the truth stares him in the face, he has the gall to say: "We must have the courage to turn our backs on it." Here was surely an instance of Barrie debunking his own reluctance to cope with unpleasant things.

In this play he concerned himself with the plight of two women who had been cruelly treated by a man. One of them has been deserted and left holding the baby, and the other has been innocent enough to suppose that her bridegroom is virtuous. Paul Digby is portrayed as a cad who has not only been unfair to these women but has shamed "the woman who bore him." Trust Barrie to bring mother into it! In the final scene when Paul asks what he can do to atone for his sins, one of his victims says, "Help unhappy women." If Barrie imagined that he was emulating Ibsen by writing a "problem" play, he must have been encouraged by some of the reviews. The *Daily Telegraph* which had been so hostile to Ibsen's plays was alarmed lest *The Wedding Guest* would encourage promiscuous seduction, and said that the play was full of "unpleasantness, painfulness

54

and doubtful morality." It was the only play by Barrie which aroused moral indignation.

Never again did he become seriously embroiled in the facts of life, and his next play *Quality Street* was far removed from reality and sordidness. He was back in the realms of romance and sentiment, where the public preferred him to be. That genteel comedy opened in September 1902 six weeks before *The Admirable Crichton*, and it went on to outrun that vastly superior play. *Little Mary* followed hard on their heels, so that no less than three plays by Barrie occupied West End theatres in 1903.

CHAPTER FOUR

WHAT THE BUTLER SAW

BARRIE WAS BORN in the same year as Anton Chekhov who will always stand head and shoulders above him in critical estimation. While it would be futile to compare their work, some coincidences may be worth noting. Both of them were of humble origin and began their literary careers by writing stories based on their mothers' reminiscences. Strict religious observance had left its mark on both writers, and they stored up impressions of Kirriemuir and Taganrog. In their schooldays they were fascinated by the theatre and indulged in amateur dramatics, and in early manhood, Chekhov was as entranced by Moscow as Barrie was by London. Neither of them found lasting happiness in marriage to actresses who had appeared in their own plays. Many more parallels could be drawn, but the contrast between their plays was far greater than anything those writers had in common. The difference was never more noticeable than in 1904 when *Peter Pan* was staged in London and *The Cherry Orchard* had its first performance in Moscow.

The wistfulness of Chekhov's characters was of an entirely different order from Barrie's vision of a "Never Never Land." At that time, however, no one realised that Barrie's work was insignificant by comparison with the great plays which were being produced in Russia. It took twenty years for Chekhov's plays to gain wide acceptance in Britain and then four of them were produced by Komisarjevsky who banished any suspicion that they were just dreary studies of boring people. The same director had considerably less success eleven years later when he produced Barrie's last play, *The Boy David.* With the exception of that strange postcript to his career, Barrie's work as a dramatist was completed before the Chekhov "craze" swept Bloomsbury.

In the first quarter of this century Barrie wrote nearly thirty plays, many of which were of no consequence. Even such an inveterate supporter as Sir John Hammerton admitted that: "We have seen his work as a dramatist attaining to its highest reach of beauty and falling more than once to a level of mediocrity to which we are almost pained to think he could ever descend." His inconsistency was clearly demonstrated in 1910 when *Old Friends* was presented on the same bill as *The Twelve Pound Look*—one of the worst pieces he ever wrote being seen alongside one of his finest achievements. *Old Friends* is about a prosperous businessman and his wife who are celebrating their daughter's engagement. The man is boasting of his success in overcoming a craving for alcohol but plies his guest with drinks from a decanter which he keeps locked in a cupboard (so as not to put temptation in the way of the servants!).

During the night, however, his darling daughter takes the keys from his pocket. It transpires that she had inherited her father's weakness for liquor. Apparently she makes a habit of sneaking downstairs in the dark to have a quiet tipple. Mother has known the dreadful secret for a long time. She has watched the evil thing leave her husband and stealthily come back to the house like a wicked old friend of the family, to take possession of the sweet and innocent girl. What are they to say to her fiance? Mother, of course, knows best. The engagement must last a year: "If all isn't well, dear, in a year's time he shall be told." She ends on a hopeful note by saying "It is just an ailment you have caught."

How could that dreadful little play have been written by the same man who created *The Twelve Pound Look* which Herbert Asquith declared was "the best short play ever written?" That exaggeration was pardonable, for the caricature of a knight ascendant must have seemed particularly amusing to Asquith in his position as Prime Minister and bestower of patronage. Others would go only as far as to say that it was the best of Barrie's short plays. It should be considered in conjunction with two longer works, *The Admirable Crichton* and *What Every Woman Knows*. Together they present a satirical view of the Edwardian social system, and it may have been those plays to which Barrie was referring when he said that he had sometimes thought that he wrote very daringly but no one had noticed it. What seemed to concern him most of all was the way in which women were treated as inferior beings. To become an appendage to a successful man was the highest honour they could hope to achieve. Maggie Wylie in *What Every Woman Knows* is prepared to settle for that, and to have the quiet satisfaction of knowing that she is largely responsible for her husband's success. Kate, in *The Twelve Pound Look* is in many respects the reverse of Maggie. She was not content to bolster up her husband's vanity by being attentive to his wishes and looking decorative. She was swaddled in luxury, not for her own sake, but because it gratified Harry Sims to see his wife being envied by other women.

While Maggie goes to great lengths to convince

John Shand that he can not do without her, Kate has taken the much bolder step of proving to herself that she can do without Harry Sims. In both cases, the women shatter their husbands' complacency—at least momentarily. The subversive quality of these plays seems to have been overlooked. H. M. Walbrook, reviewing *The Twelve Pound Look* in his study of *J. M. Barrie and the Theatre* even took the same attitude as Harry Sims. "After all" he wrote, "he was not a bad husband as husbands go. At any rate he made a handsome home for his wife, gave her all she could desire on the material side, and philandered with no other women. A wife able to put a little brain into her love could have made a good deal of such a partner."

Walbrook's essay was written in 1922, twelve years after the first production of the play, and yet the message had not penetrated the fools' paradise where men held sway. Women who ran away from successful men were still regarded as fools or cowards, and it was their own fault if marriage failed to satisfy them. By these standards Maggie Wylie's behaviour was acceptable for she certainly used her brain to come to terms with John Shand. It does not seem to have been considered highly immoral for her to actively encourage her husband to spend three weeks in the company of the beautiful girl he professed to adore. Maggie may have been confident that they would soon lose interest in each other, but her scheme was daring, if not scandalous. And yet there was something inherently prim and respectable about both Maggie and Kate which made their actions seem more amusing than adventurous, with the result that they have not come to be regarded as champions of female emancipation. They were, however, ladies of very advanced ideas for their time. At least they were prepared to defy convention—unlike Lady Mary Lasenby in *The Admirable Crichton*. She might seem to be the most despicable of all Barrie's heroines, forsaking the man she loves simply because he has suffered a set-back in his social status. She is also the most pitiable, for she is the prisoner of a system that decrees she must marry someone of equal rank.

Lady Mary recognises that "There is something wrong with England" but she is incapable of doing anything to rectify its faults. She knows that Crichton, the butler, is a far stronger and abler man than the fatuous Lord Brocklehurst with whom she is condemned to live. Her last words to Crichton are: "Tell me one thing: you have not lost your courage?" to which he replies, "No, my lady." He might have added "But *you* have" were it not for the fact that he thoroughly approves of the social system which keeps them apart. He regards class distinction as the most natural thing in the world and has demonstrated that, even on a desert island, there can be no such thing as equality. The masters and servants may merely exchange places. The play presents the argument for what is now termed "meritocracy" and it is extraordinary that such a discerning critic as William Archer should have thought that Barrie had stumbled only by accident upon a revolutionare theme. Archer doubted whether Barrie had the least idea of the immensity of his attack upon the constituted social order of the realm.

The onslaught may not have been quite so devastating as Archer suggested, but it seems clear that Barrie had a higher regard for ability than nobility. It was a theme to which he returned in *What Every Woman Knows* where Venables observes that it is not enough for John Shand's speeches to be as good as those of the patricians. He had to do better. Of course Barrie was much too fond of High Society to have any desire to overthrow it. He simply wanted its privileges to be more widely enjoyed. There could be no objection to people living in the lap of luxury if they had made some effort to get there. He was so diligent himself that it must have dismayed him to see the best things in life being wasted upon a lethargic aristocracy.

In the first act of *The Admirable Crichton* he created an impression of languid boredom that was akin to Chekhov's world but the three sisters in Barrie's comedy are utterly frivolous creatures, exhausted by the strain of deciding which frocks to take on a cruise, or by trying on engagement rings. Ernest, their brother, has nothing better to do than to toy with epigrams, and cricket is the only accomplishment of Treherne, the young clergyman who is attached to one of the girls. Another suitor, Lord Brocklehurst, is devoid of any skills and can not even do a simple conjuring trick to amuse the lower classes. "It's a pity" says his prospective father-in-law, the Earl of Loam, "Every one in our position ought to be able to do something."

Loam is the most ridiculous of all these superior creatures for he deludes himself that he is enlightened and prides himself on being an intellectual aristocrat of radical views. He professes to yearn for the day when social barriers are swept away but consoles himself with the thought that "That is entirely and utterly out of the question." Until the millennium dawns, the lower orders must be content with the monthly tea parties which he gives, under the impression that he is treating his servants as equals. Whilst warning his daughters not to betray the least sign of condescension, Loam makes the staff squirm with embarrassment by referring to them as his "valued friends." No one is more appalled by his lordship's behaviour than Crichton who wants everyone kept in his place.

Crichton's definition of a "tweeny" shows his pride in the ramifications of the system: "That is to say, my lady, she is not at present, strictly speaking anything; a between maid; she helps the vegetable maid. It is she, my lady, who conveys the dishes from one end of the kitchen table, where they are placed by the cook, to the other end, where they enter into the charge of Thomas and John" (the footmen). Barrie, who was brought up to think that a house with one servant was the height of luxury, must have been amazed to discover the vast establishments which were maintained in Mayfair.

The obsequious English butler, at the head of a pyramid of servants, was a figure that fascinated Barrie. Crichton was not the only one he invented. Matey has a fairly substantial part to play in *Dear Brutus* and Dolphin is a dominant figure in *Shall We Join The Ladies?* though he does not utter a word. In his introduction to the latter play, Barrie gave a vivid impression of the imperturbable manner of the perfect butler. In explaining that the guests at Sam Smith's dinner party are being served with fruit by Dolphin, Barrie says, "The only other attendant is a maid in the background, as for an emergency, and she is as interested in the conversation as he is indifferent to it. If one of the guests were to destroy himself, Dolphin would merely sign for her to remove the debris while he continued to serve the fruit."

One of the best jokes that Barrie perpetrated was to pretend that *Shall We Join The Ladies?* was the first act of an unfinished play. Most critics took him at his word and speculated as to how the situation might have developed. Sir John Hammerton was one of the minority who doubted if the author ever had any intention of finishing it—"because" he said, "it seems improbable to me that even the genius of a Barrie could have maintained the interest awakened by the first act with any dramatic force throughout three more. Rather does it belong to the order of stories that leave their hearers entirely in the air, and have no denouement because the original proposition would be destroyed in any attempt to carry it to a logical conclusion." Dennis Mackail, in his massive biography of Barrie, put it more bluntly, saying that "It was unfinished because he couldn't finish it." A. E. Wilson left the options open: "Whether it was just a brilliant jeu d'esprit or whether Barrie ever intended to complete it remains a fascinating unsolved mystery of the theatre."

The solution to that mystery is to be found in a letter which Barrie wrote to Mrs E. V. Lucas on February 27, 1921, exactly three months before the first performance of *Shall We Join The Ladies?* In that letter he stated: "I am writing a one-act play in which all the company are seated at dinner." That would seem to be conclusive evidence that he never had any intention of prolonging the play and revealing how Sam Smith identified his brother's murderer. The play is not a "whodunnit" but a shrewd and amusing study of people whose consciences are troubling them. It does not matter which of the guests at Sam Smith's dinner party committed murder at Monte Carlo. The point is that they are all guilty of something, and they are all incapable of proving their innocence. Each of them had done something which could prove to be incriminating, and so everyone becomes entangled in a web of suspicion.

The play was chosen to open the theatre of the Royal Academy of Dramatic Art where it was performed by a glittering cast including Dion Boucicault, Fay Compton, Charles Hawtrey, Sybil Thorndike, Cyril Maude, Lady Tree, Leon Quartermaine, Lillah McCarthy, Sir Johnston Forbes-Robertson, Irene Vanbrugh and Marie Lohr. The silent butler was played by Gerald du Maurier, the original John Shand, and Hilda Trevelyan, who created the role of Maggie, appeared as the maid who has only one line to speak. There was another charity performance later in the same year. With a different cast, it went in as a curtain-raiser to Galsworthy's *Loyalties* at St Martin's Theatre and they ran together for 407 performances. It is long overdue for revival.

The central character, Sam Smith, is very similar to the impish Lob in *Dear Brutus*. He, too, is entertaining a group of people who wonder what it is they have in common and why they have been invited to spend a week at his house. Smith is likened to "an elderly Cupid" or "a pocket edition of Pickwick" whereas Lob answers to the description of a gnome, and a petulant one at that. Both of these mischievous hosts could well be caricatures of the playwright himself. It may be significant that Barrie told Mrs Lucas he was writing *Shall We Join the Ladies?* at the same time as he was planning to give a real dinner party—"and I quite mix up who is to be at which."

Smith's after-dinner speech begins amiably enough but very casually he drifts round to the subject of his brother who died in mysterious circumstances in Monte Carlo two years previously. After some inquiries Smith became convinced that his brother had been poisoned. All the people who may have had some motive for killing him and who had been in Monte Carlo at the time were eventually tracked down. "I invited them to my house for a week," says Smith, "and they are all sitting round my table this evening." The guests are dumbfounded but when they recover their powers of speech they are indignant. "You are not all turning against me, are you?" Smith blandly inquires. "I assure you I don't accuse any of you yet. I know that one of you did it, but I am not sure which one. I shall know soon." Pressed to reveal when he intends to make his accusation, he says that it will be soon after the men rejoin the ladies after dinner. Of course the play ends before that happens —the last line providing the title. As the men rise from the table, a woman's scream is heard from the next room and Dolphin reappears in a very agitated state which is quite out of character for him. The curtain descends before we can discover what the butler saw.

Among many questions left unanswered is why Smith compelled the guests to retire to Dolphin's room instead of the drawing-room. Could this be the equivalent to Lob's Wood in *Dear Brutus*—a place where people are given a second chance in life, or at least an opportunity to expiate whatever sins they may have committed? If that were the case, it is just as well that *Shall We Join The Ladies?* did not go beyond the first act. One Lob's Wood is more than enough. That scene in *Dear Brutus* has often been held up as the supreme example of Barrie's artistry but its poignancy is cleverly contrived rather than heartfelt. One of the first critics to say a word against it was James Agate, reviewing the second London production in 1922. He said that he did not find his sensibility greatly touched although the acting of Gerald du Maurier and Faith Celli had a dream-like quality. "The material" said Agate, "was just not good enough."

Dear Brutus had its first performance in October 1917 when thousands of young men were dying on the ridge of Passchendaele and Russia was on the verge of revolution. Europe was in turmoil, but London audiences were contentedly lapping up the milk-sops which Barrie offered them, and shedding tears over Margaret Dearth, the insufferably sweet little girl who "might have been." The long duet between Margaret and her father has some beautifully tender moments but the joy they derive from being in each other's company does not seem so much spontaneous as superimposed. They flutter around from one sentimental epigram to the next. "To be very gay, dearest dear, is so near to being very sad" is at least preferable to Mr Dearth's assertion that "The laugh that children are born with lasts just so long as they have perfect faith."

Barrie's chronic weakness for investing inanimate objects with human characteristics is seen at its worst in *Dear Brutus* when Lob addresses some limp flowers as if they were babies that had tumbled out of their cots: "Pretty, pretty, let me see where you have a pain." Presumably this is what Agate meant by saying that Barrie had "a passion for literary baby-ribbons." It is astonishing that W. A. Darlington could say of *Dear Brutus* that, except for one or two passages which would be easy to cut or amend, "there is nothing in it of sentimentality." The entire moonlight serenade of the

Dearths is sentimental, as is the cosy relationship between Mr and Mrs Coade, to mention but two of the many purple passages. Other critics have claimed that "there is not a single jarring note" in the play and one even went so far as to say that "the sentiment has philosophic warranty."

By comparison with *The Admirable Crichton* or *What Every Woman Knows*, it seems a florid play, overadorned with "insights" into human nature. The characters are puppets who simply illustrate various patterns of behaviour. There are those who would always take the wrong turning in life if they were given a second chance, and there are others who would redeem themselves. Finally there are people like the Coades who could never be anything but nice. Old Solomon Caw in *The Little White Bird* could have saved him the trouble of writing *Dear Brutus*. "In this world" said Caw, "there are no second chances." Barrie was forever opening windows on another world, however. It was through a window that John Shand stole each night in his quest for enlightenment, and through another window Peter and Wendy flew to a land of enchantment. Mary Rose entered through a window and Lob pushed his guests out of a French window. Above all, Barrie was never to forget his mother sitting at a window in Thrums.

Chapter Five

"IT'S NO' NATURAL"

BOTH OF JAMES BARRIE'S parents were over forty when he was born and his brother, Alex., was old enough to be his father. It was Alex who took a paternal interest in his education while David Barrie seems to have treated the boy as if he were his grandson. Respectful references to the God-fearing weaver are to be found in some of the books but there is a curious air of detachment. No mention is made of any fatherly attributes. He had been a devoted husband to Margaret Ogilvy and that was all that mattered. "Did you ever notice what an extraordinary woman your mother is?" he asked James, who spent his life answering that question in the affirmative.

Margaret Ogilvy was the inspiration and the ruination of his literary career. The early stories were based on her recollections and the rest of his work was founded upon recollections of her. His excessive admiration for his mother developed into an obsession with motherhood in general. At one time, this may have enhanced the value of his writings but, in the long run, it has been their undoing. By constantly dwelling on the maternal theme, Barrie exposed the fundamental weakness of his own nature. It is a terrible reflection on the critics of that time that he had to wait until he was sixty to be told that his work lacked robustness. "I haven't seen it put exactly thus before," he wrote to Lady Cynthia Asquith in 1920, when he received the New York reviews of *Mary Rose*. "Why can't I be more robust?" he asked. "You see how it rankles."

Ten years later, Sir John Hammerton remarked upon the "sexlessness" of Barrie's work: "In all that he has written, despite the continuous harping upon the idea of motherhood and mothering, there is probably less of what we know as 'sex appeal' than in any other novelist or dramatist." Hammerton took *Peter Pan* as an example and said, "The fact that he has never been represented on the stage except by girls and women does seem to suggest a lack of virility." Other critics were to say the same about *The Boy David*. W. A. Darlington observed that "in all Barrie's writings there is hardly to be remembered a scene between husband and wife that goes beneath the surface, while the many scenes between mothers and sons, and the exquisitely written father and daughter scene in *Dear Brutus* are all deeply and truly felt."

Darlington omitted to mention yet another variation on the theme of love which is to be found in Barrie's plays—the illicit affairs between married men and beautiful women. Erring husbands were always made to look ridiculous. They were so captivated by the charms of other women that they failed to appreciate the estimable qualities of their own wives. John Shand in *What Every Woman Knows* and Purdie in *Dear Brutus* were identical in this respect and their declarations of love for Lady Sybil and Joanna Trout are so alike that they could be interchangeable. In both cases, the wives' suspicions are aroused by their husbands' efforts to appear more affectionate! Maggie says, "Many a kindly little thing he has done for me that he didn't use to do" and when Purdie is speaking to Joanna about his wife, he says, "I think she has some sort of idea now that when I give her anything nice it means that you have been nice to me."

Barrie made all philanderers appear to be the same. His romantic ideal was a "kind, beaming smile that children could warm their hands at." Love, in any physical sense, was out of the question. It is impossible to imagine any of the couples in his plays embracing each other with any passion. They may, like Mrs Coade, put a muffler round her husband's neck as a supreme gesture of affection or, like Mary Rose, playfully throw a butter-dish at the father of her child. Crichton's proposal of marriage to Lady Mary Lasenby must rank among the most ludicrous in the annals of drama: "I have grown to love you; are you afraid to mate with me?" When she asks him to say what was the first time that he thought she was nicer than the other girls, he strokes her hair and says: "We were chasing goats on the Big Slopes, and you out-distanced us all; you were the first of our party to run a goat down; I was proud of you that day." That is the most extraordinary admission of Barrie's fondness for tom-boyish qualities, and Peter Pan and the Boy David possessed them in full measure.

Darlington was charitable enough to suggest that Barrie was "temperamentally" unfitted for married life, but it is now widely assumed that he was sexually impotent. The heroines of his plays were either boyish or maternal. The heroine of his life was not Mary Ansell whom he married, but Margaret Ogilvy who gave birth to him. He was like Jamie in *A Window in Thrums* who tells Jess: "Oh, mother, I carry aboot yer face wi' me aye; an' sometimes at nicht I kind o' greet to think o' ye."

71

In *The Little Minister* Gavin Dishart makes a similar confession. When he protests that he would not allow any face to influence him, his mother says: "Ah, Gavin, I'm thinking I'm the reason you pay so little regard to women's faces. It's no' natural." Gavin's reply would appear to sum up the author's plight: "You've spoilt me, you see, mother, for ever caring for another woman. I would compare her to you and then where would she be?" The character of Margaret in *The Little Minister* was so clearly modelled on Barrie's mother that it is surprising he discarded her when he adapted the novel for the stage. Possibly it was that omission which convinced him in later years that the dramatised version was very much inferior to the original.

Professor James Roy credited Barrie with having created a new type of heroine—the motherly woman. Roy said, "It is not so much love between men and women as the comedy and tragedy of the maternal instinct that interests Barrie." If there were no more to it than that, then it might be acceptable, but unfortunately Barrie made no clear distinction between the two forms of love. His characters could be romantic and maternal at the same time. This was bad enough where they were, in fact, mothers and sons like Jess and Jamie in *A Window in Thrums* and Margaret and Gavin in *The Little Minister* but it became embarrassing when Tommy and Grizel and Peter and Wendy doted upon each other in the same way.

One of the most interesting of all the mothers manquée in Barrie's work is Mrs Dowey, the Scots charwoman in *The Old Lady Shows Her Medals*. She is supposed to have been modelled on a landlady he had as a student in Edinburgh, and not on Margaret Ogilvy, and this may account for her being refreshingly different from most of the maternal characters in his plays. Mrs Dowey boasts to her friends that she has a son fighting with the Black Watch on the Western Front, and she clutches a bundle of censored letters to prove it. The other women are highly sceptical until the stalwart soldier turns up one day. Mrs Dowey had "adopted" him at random, so that she did not feel left out of the war effort, and had sent him parcels of food and comforts. The soldier cheerfully exploits her generosity. It is to their mutual advantage to keep up the pretence that he is Mrs Dowey's son, but gradually he becomes as genuinely fond of her as she is proud of him.

The rough and sinewy Private Dewey was the precursor of Harry, the rugged Australian soldier in *Mary Rose*. In that play, however, the mother and son relationship is much more ambiguously handled with the ghost of Mary Rose having a child-like innocence which makes her seem younger than Harry. They are more like lovers than mother and son, but of course Mary Rose always had the peculiar ambition of wanting to sit on her son's knee! No play of Barrie's was more whimsical and elusive—the two adjectives which he implored critics to desist from using in relation to his work. He may have borrowed this play's theme from James Hogg's *Kilmeny*, but the sentimental trimmings were all his own work. On "The Island Which Likes to be Visited," Mary Rose addresses a tree stump as "my ownest seat, how I have missed you" just as Margaret Dearth in *Dear Brutus* goes into raptures about a little pool of water which she calls "such a darling mirror." Both plays are full of the poignancy of parting but Mary Rose and Margaret Dearth carefully pave the way for their departure. The latter is reluctant to let her father out of her sight, lest they should never meet again, and Mary Rose says, "Don't you think the sad thing is that we seldom know when the last time has come? We could make so much more of it." Barrie certainly made the most of that sweet sorrow. He shrank, however, from suggesting that his heroines did anything so drastic and irreversible as dying. They simply vanished into thin air and that was typical of Barrie's approach to tragedy and grief. Writing about the death of W. E. Henley's little daughter he said, "That lovely child died when she was about five. One might call it a sudden idea that came to her in the middle of her romping."

Mary Rose finally vanishes like Peter Pan: "The smallest star shoots down for her, and with her arms stretched forth to it trustingly she walks out through the window into the empyrean." Fortunately, the play is not entirely swaddled in sentimentality and it has at least two very interesting characters—Mrs Otery, the taciturn housekeeper, and Cameron, the divinity student who acts as a ghillie during the vacation. Most of Barrie's Scottish characters are Lowlanders but Cameron is a true Celt who strikes a balance between pride and servility summed up in the phrase "In saying I am your humble servant I do not imply that I am not as good as you are." Cameron is like John Shand in that he regards education as "the grandest thing in the world." He makes many wise observations in the play but it is Harry who speaks the most famous lines: "There are worse things than not finding what you are looking for; there is finding them so different from what you had hoped."

That was also the theme of *Quality Street* in which Barrie related how an officer returned from the Napoleonic wars and found that he was unable to recognise the girl he had left behind. It is a romantic comedy of delicate charm but the sisters, Susan and Phoebe Throssel, would seem to be made of porcelain rather than flesh and blood. They are fragile, artificial creatures. The most substantial and convincing of all Barrie's heroines was Maggie Wylie in *What Every Woman Knows* and some cynics have said that this was the best portrait he ever drew of his mother. Margaret Ogilvy certainly appeared in many guises, but she is seen in all her homely glory in the book which bears her name.

The very idea of a man revealing his innermost feelings for his mother was repugnant to many of Barrie's fellow-countrymen and J. H. Millar described that book as "an exercise compared with which the labours of the resurrectionist are praiseworthy." Most English critics took a much more favourable view of it and it has been called "the most beautiful tribute ever paid by a son to the memory of his dead mother." Barrie began the last chapter by saying: "For years I had been trying to prepare myself for my mother's death, trying to foresee how she would die, seeing myself when she was dead. Even then I knew it was a vain thing I did, but I am sure there was no morbidness in it."

If he did not consider that to be morbid, then it is hardly surprising that he had no qualms about publishing an intimate account of his devotion to her, and the pitiful frailty of her last days. It would appear that he wrote *Margaret Ogilvy* to atone for not having been at her side when the end came. He was left to imagine "the ineffable

75

glow of motherhood" which lit up her features and yet, for all its mawkishness, the book has some remarkable qualities. As a character study and as a chronicle of the domestic dignity of Victorian Scotland, it continues to be of great interest and value.

In the same year that Barrie paid his respects to his mother, he dedicated a book to Mary Ansell. *Sentimental Tommy* was the only work which bore her name and it is significant that there was no inscription on its sequel, *Tommy and Grizel*, which was published four years later. By that time his marriage had lost any romantic flavour that it ever had and the character of Grizel was not modelled on Mary Ansell or, for that matter, Margaret Ogilvy. The inspiration was Sylvia Llewelyn Davies, mother of the boys to whom Barrie became so devoted. He made no secret of the resemblance and even told Bernard Partridge, who illustrated the book, that Grizel should look like Mrs Llewelyn Davies, in whose company he spent so much of his time.

That novel contained one of Barrie's most anguished admissions: "He gave her all his affection, but his passion, like an outlaw, had ever to hunt alone." Though it has been described as the finest and most mature of all the Thrums books, it is a perplexing piece of work. In it there is a reference to sentimentality being a "leering, distorted thing" but no matter how hard Barrie may have tried to avoid its clutches, he was its slave for life.

CHAPTER SIX

THE HOMECOMING

ONLY ONE PLAY by Scotland's most successful dramatist had its first performance in his native land. That was *The Boy David* which opened at the King's Theatre, Edinburgh, on November 21, 1936. That production went on to meet its doom in London, predeceasing the author by four months. It was the brain-child of his old age.

A strange Biblical drama, it was quite unlike anything else he had written although it resembled *Peter Pan* to the extent that the young hero was portrayed by an actress. The play was less dramatic than the circumstances under which it was produced. Some of the details have been related by Denis Mackail, Lady Cynthia Asquith and Janet Dunbar in their biographies of Barrie, but the irony of that homecoming has not been fully appreciated.

The one play to which his fellow-countrymen paid effusive tribute turned out to be the greatest disaster of his career, leaving him with the bitter taste of failure at the end of his days. It was not a "flop" in the normal sense. Nearly 20,000 people saw the play in Edinburgh and about three times that number in London, but Barrie seems to have believed that it was his masterpiece and he was shattered to discover that this view was not widely shared. It was because he had aimed so high that he was deeply hurt by the production's failure to

77

live up to his aspirations and by the critics' inability to recognise the play's latent qualities.

The damage to his self-respect had been done by the time that it was decided to take the play off after fifty-six performances at His Majesty's Theatre, and he could put a brave face on the final indignity. Shortly before the closure, he wrote to Cynthia Asquith: "Probably it is not what the great public cares for. I am not depressed for myself and know it is only one of the pinpricks, but I grieve for Miss Bergner." In a post-script he noted that Elisabeth Bergner, for whom he had written the play, had looked in to see him on her way to the theatre and had "taken an oath against bitterness." Barrie must have made a similar vow. He had always been a shrewd judge of public taste and yet here he was shrugging off his failure to captivate audiences as if it did not worry him. Harley Granville-Barker was nearer the truth when he said that Barrie did not complain openly. "That was not his way, but the grief struck the deeper."

Miss Bergner, an Austrian actress who was making a name for herself on the London stage and in the cinema, had first impressed him with her portrayal of a fourteen-year-old girl in *Escape Me Never*. She told Barrie that she was looking for a more complex part and the old dramatist, who was warming to the idea of writing a play specially for her, is reputed to have suggested Mary Queen of Scots as a suitable subject.

Miss Bergner may have felt that she had neither the right physique nor an appropriate accent for that role, and may have stated a preference for a Jewish part. It could have been only through associating Barrie with *Peter Pan* that she hit upon the notion of playing David, the giant-killer. No actress familiar with the wide range of Barrie's work would have dreamt of asking him to write a play about a boy. The idea appealed to him, however, and three months after Barrie's first meeting with Miss Bergner, he was happily immersed in writing the play and he mentioned in a letter to Cynthia Asquith: "I managed to slay Goliath at ten minutes past six." After thirteen years' abstinence from play-writing his enthusiasm for the stage had been re-kindled.

He had probably completed the play by June of that year (1934) when *The Times* reported that "Sir James Barrie is writing a three-act play for Miss Elisabeth Bergner for production in London early next year. Miss Bergner has discussed the matter with Sir James Barrie and has even offered to overcome the language difficulty if it should be found necessary for her to speak Scots. The draft of the play, however, provides her with an English-speaking part."

Over two years were to elapse before the play was staged. The first delay was caused by Miss Bergner's film commitments, and it was not until the autumn of 1935 that C. B. Cochran announced that she would appear in a play "about David and Goliath." Cochran had commissioned Augustus John to design the scenery and William Walton to compose the music. Sir John Martin-Harvey, Godfrey Tearle and Leon Quartermaine had been engaged for leading roles. Nina Boucicault and Hilda Trevelyan (the original Peter and Wendy) had been considered for the part of David's mother, but the final choice was the Scots actress, Jean Cadell.

One of the things about the story of David which greatly intrigued Barrie was that, in all the records of this illustrious man, there was no reference to his mother.

Barrie, who had written a book about his own mother, and who had been obsessed with motherhood all his life, was amazed to discover this omission in the annals of David. He atoned for the negligence of the ancient scribes by giving David's mother a prominent place in the play, leaving it to Samuel to tell her, "In all his mighty history, you will have no share. No record will remain; even of the *name* of the mother of David."

The first word spoken by David in the play is "Mother!" It is followed by that memorable line, "Mother, I have killed a lion" echoing Michael's boast in *Peter Pan*: "Wendy, I've killed a pirate!"

In January 1936, only a month before the play was due to open in Edinburgh for a preliminary run of a fortnight, its provisional title was announced. It was to be called *The Two Shepherds*. Barrie's first inclination had been to call it *The Two Farmers*. Without even knowing the title, the public eagerly bought tickets for the first performance, paying what was then the princely sum of a guinea for a seat in the stalls. Then, in the first few weeks of 1936, Barrie's world began to fall apart. Rudyard Kipling, his successor as Rector of St Andrews University, died on January 18 and two days later came the death of King George V, and Edward VIII acceded to the throne. The play's Edinburgh opening was postponed for a month. On February 10, the day on which rehearsals were due to begin, Barrie's sister Margaret died, leaving him the sole survivor of Margaret Ogilvy's ten children. He was in such poor health that he could not go regularly to rehearsals and he was disheartened by the little that he did see of them.

On the day that Cochran announced that advance bookings for the Edinburgh fortnight amounted to £7000 and that the play would be known as *The Boy David*, Elisabeth Bergner collapsed with acute appendicitis. The production had to be postponed indefinitely and Cochran had to refund all the money that had been taken at the Edinburgh and London box-offices. It had been used to pay the wages of a hundred-strong company and to build the settings. Rehearsals were not resumed for seven months by which time Theodore Komisarjevsky, one of Europe's most renowned producers, had been engaged to direct the play. His imaginative production of *King Lear* had been acclaimed at Stratford earlier that year and he was famed for directing Chekhov's plays.

On November 17, after four weeks' rehearsals in London, the company travelled to Edinburgh. For the last time in his life, Barrie set out from King's Cross to return to Scotland and he was no longer the lonely passenger who had been familiar with that route for half a century. On this occasion he had over a hundred followers who had three days in which to adjust the production to the King's Theatre and make final preparations for the first night.

The Scotsman was treating it as the most momentous event in Scottish theatrical history. Barrie was too ill to leave his room in the Caledonian Hotel and did not wish to have a photograph taken of him, but *The Scotsman* reproduced an early portrait of him by Sir William Nicholson. In *The Greenwood Hat* which he wrote in 1930, Barrie said that it was his "only boast" that he had never been interviewed but he made an exception to this rule on the eve of the premiere of *The Boy David*. He spoke about the play to J. W. Herries of *The Scotsman* and an account of that conversation was published on November 21.

It would seem that the playwright was anxious to make it clear that the principal theme of the play was not the conflict between David and Goliath. This was the aspect which had dominated all the advance publicity and, while it may have been good for business, it was very misleading. After pointing out that it was not "a romantic play of dramatic action" between David and Goliath, Herries stated that it was "an inquiry into the elements of difference in the characters of Saul and David."

"David was always forgiven. He got off lightly for his misdeeds. Saul, on the other hand, always seemed to suffer the uttermost penalties for his sins and shortcomings." Herries went on to quote Barrie as saying that it was an extraordinary and impressive thing how the Lord seemed to single out these two men, both shepherds, and made them great figures in history.

We have Barrie's own word for it that this was an accurate summary of his views, for he wrote to Mrs Herries the next day: "I thought your husband's piece in yesterday's *Scotsman* an astonishingly correct interpretation of the words I had said to him about my play." The only press interview of his career had worked out to his satisfaction and it is surprising that the gist of it has not been included in any of the volumes containing the text of the play. Barrie died before he could amend and adorn the text for publication and so it is mercifully free from his usual whimsical afterthoughts, but it is also devoid of any explanatory notes. If he had overseen its publication, it is more than likely that the title would have reverted to *The Two Shepherds* which may have been less dramatic than *The Boy David* but corresponded more closely to the theme.

Barrie did not entirely discount the spectacular theatrical attributes of the duel between David and Goliath, and he wanted it to happen on-stage so that the audience could see the mighty fall. This was attempted at the first performance in Edinburgh but it was so cumbersome and ineffective that the giant was turned into a disembodied voice, and was slain off-stage in London. That alteration was one of several which he had to authorise without seeing the play performed. He was confined to his hotel for two weeks, apart from visiting hospitals to be X-rayed.

On the day that the play opened, *The Scotsman* reported that "Sir James Barrie has recently been suffering from a slight attack of rheumatism; but he has no fear of any set-back from the eager air of Edinburgh." It quoted him as saying, "I feel I am in my home town, and the east wind always seems to invigorate me" but on this occasion it failed to have any therapeutic effect. Most people in the first night audience were unaware that he was too ill to go to the theatre, and they assumed that he was there, lurking in the corner of a box. When the performance ended and the company were taking the curtain calls, there were loud cries of "Author." Finally, Elisabeth Bergner stepped forward and said, "I have the honour to express Sir James Barrie's gratitude." He had missed the finale to an amazing career and never had the satisfaction of being acclaimed in a Scottish theatre.

He had the consolation of being treated as a national hero by *The Scotsman* which gave as much prominence to the advent of *The Boy David* as it did, two weeks later, to the abdication of King Edward. Pride of place on the main news page was given to an enthusiastic review of the play and it occupied two and a half broad columns. There was a leader paying homage to Barrie and a full page of pictures. Those ten photographs, taken from the grand circle during the performance with nothing but stage lighting to assist the cameraman, are so blurred and distant that one may glean little from them. The London papers also carried reports of the occasion but no reviews, owing to the convention that Fleet Street critics should wait until plays reached the West End. The advance reports were, however, sufficiently coloured to suggest that *The Boy David* was not up to Barrie's usual standards. These were the first ominous rumblings of disappointment, which finally engulfed the play when it reached His Majesty's Theatre. Even *The Scotsman* which had displayed so much respect for it in Edinburgh, published a much cooler assessment of it in London.

It seems that Barrie was not so disappointed by what was said about the play as by what was left unsaid. He was particularly hurt by the review in *The Times* which described the dresses and hair ornaments worn by the grand ladies in the audience. It was obvious that the critic was more impressed by the occasion than by the play itself. It had been running in London for over a week before Barrie was well enough to attend a performance. Denis Mackail has recorded that "He hated the whole evening" and it is clear from a letter that he wrote to Lady Cynthia Asquith that he registered several complaints with the producer. He had been assured by Miss Bergner that "all those changes in the third act have now been made" and he added, "All those things and others could have been done in Edinburgh." In that same letter, written more than a month after the play opened at the King's Theatre, he made the highly significant statement that: "Miss Bergner says that on Wednesday evening she gave her first real performance as David and enthused herself as well as the audience." As he was not present on that occasion, and is reputed to have been depressed by the only performance which he did attend, it is puzzling that he should have left £2000 to Miss Bergner "for the best performance ever given in any play of mine." Having written the play for her, he must have felt responsible for the damage which it may have done to her reputation.

Apparently Miss Bergner shared Cynthia Asquith's conviction that the adult David—the David of the visions—should have been played by a man. Most critics would go further and prefer the entire role to be more masculine. As W. A. Darlington observed, "In the hero of such a tale, virility is the first quality that is needed. Barrie knew that well enough for Saul has it in full measure." That part was, from all accounts, superbly played by Godfrey Tearle, but Darlington continued, "How then, can the hero of the tale be acted by a woman? How can he be turned into a wistful, sexless creature, own brother to Peter Pan, without allowing the tale to dwindle?"

Three aspects of the play have been admired by some critics—David's mixture of audacity and doubt in the first act, his encounter with Saul in the second act, and the final scene with Jonathan. It is all couched in pseudo-Biblical language and Barrie laid some emphasis on the need to perform it "with Israelite excess of voice and gesture." This emotional exuberance was to be shown at times by all the characters in the play, but he specified that the last scene should be "an idyll of quiet rural loveliness, in contrast with the rest of the play." He even suggested that there should be some real sheep grazing on the stage, and of course there had to be an ass for David to ride upon.

Barrie was greatly exercised over details like the shape of the rock on which David stood, balancing a spear on his shoulders, at the end of the play. He was convinced that neither the director nor the designer understood the significance of that rock in which David had his little cave, and they are not the only people who have wondered why he attached so much importance to it.

Of all the background notes, none is more intriguing than the comment which follows Samuel's recognition of David's powers: "Samuel is experiencing the loveliest thrill of a craftsman, the sudden meeting with another in childhood." It would be interesting to know which budding genius had once had this effect on Barrie.

His own powers were failing by the time he wrote this play and yet he set his sights higher than he had ever done before. It had its last performance at the end of January 1937, and he knew that it was the end of his career. The future held the prospect of only one "awfully big adventure," on which he embarked in June of that year.

The first radio broadcast of any of his work—a production of *Dear Brutus*—was heard later that year. It is surprising that he was so reluctant to permit his plays to be performed on the radio when it would seem that he had no objections to them being turned into musical comedies. *Quality Street* became *Phoebe* and *The Little Minister* became *Wild Grows the Heather*. Several of his plays were filmed, and the first screen version of *The Admirable Crichton* suffered the ludicrous

86

indignity of being called *Male and Female*. Barrie agreed that Charlie Chaplin should play Peter Pan but that dream was never fulfilled. Peter Pan, however, became the subject of a Walt Disney cartoon and, much more recently, it had the misfortune to be turned into a sugar-candy musical on television with Danny Kaye as a benign Captain Hook. Barrie's work has always been popular in America. On his first visit to the United States (in 1895) he was accompanied by Robertson Nicoll and he met Charles Frohman—the two men who did so much to promote his career as a writer. During that visit he was entertained to dinner by a large assembly of New York publishers and on the menu was "Haggis à la Thrums."

Margaret Ogilvy's boy was well on the way to becoming another Immortal Memory—but not in his native land, where his reputation reached its peak in 1936 and never really recovered from the anti-climax of *The Boy David*. It is a sign of that disenchantment that, for thirty years, the Edinburgh International Festival has ignored the existence of the most successful Scottish playwright. It could make amends for this neglect by presenting three or four short pieces in a single evening.

In the last quarter of the twentieth century, Barrie's excursions to Never-Never Land, Lob's Wood, and The Island That Likes to be Visited, may have lost much of their appeal but the vigour of some of his short plays and stories is undiminished. *Ibsen's Ghosts*, *The Twelve-Pound Look* and *Shall We Join The Ladies?* would make a glorious triple bill. The first act of *What Every Woman Knows* could stand on its own—a perfect little comedy about a Scotsman on the make and the woman who was the making of him. Barrie was completely at ease in that scene in the living-room of the Wylies' house and every line that was spoken was like a move on the dambrod. He had it all cunningly mapped out and had the audience completely at his mercy. When the play was revived in London in 1974, and at Pitlochry in 1976, the critics were utterly disarmed by the humour and the consummate craftsmanship of the opening scene. Anyone who saw either of these productions would realise that J. M. Barrie was far from being a spent force.

CHAPTER SEVEN

"FRAGMENTS OF IMMORTALITY"

CHARLES VENABLES, the patronising Cabinet Minister in *What Every Woman Knows*, remarked that the Scots were such a mixture of the practical and the emotional that they escaped out of an Englishman's hand like a trout. No doubt Barrie had heard himself described in these terms, for they would seem to be particularly applicable to him. He revealed exactly that combination of qualities in his dedication of *Peter Pan* to the Llewellyn Davies boys when he said that he could not remember whether his impulse to write the play "was a last desperate throw to retain the five of you for a little longer, or merely a cold decision to turn you into bread and butter."

He must have been even more torn between sentiment and commerce when he wrote *Margaret Ogilvy*, cherishing fond memories of his mother and, at the same time, profiting from them. Many biographers and critics have found it so difficult to reconcile the astute and the tender aspects of his nature that he has eluded their grasp. They have either succumbed to the spell which he cast over them or they have violently recoiled from it. In his lifetime he had many more admirers than denigrators but the ratio is now reversed. It is difficult to have much respect for a writer who could, for instance, describe "How my mother got her soft face" or who could make Mary Rose say: "You know, the loveliest thing in the world is the navy, and the loveliest thing in the navy is H.M.S. Valiant, and the loveliest thing on

H.M.S. Valiant is Lieutenant Simon Sobersides, and the loveliest thing on Lieutenant Simon Sobersides is the little tuft of hair which will keep standing up at the back of his head."

Such twaddle, masquerading as expressions of affection and tenderness, defiles far too much of Barrie's work. The reader or spectator may be cheerfully striding along the Barrie trail only to discover that it is littered with puddles of sentimentality through which he has to squelch. Not many of his plays and even fewer of his books are devoid of such pitfalls. As well as writing much that now seems to be totally inconsequential, Barrie tarnished some of his finest efforts.

Even the greatest dramatists have occasionally fallen from grace but, in Barrie's case, the variation in quality is so extreme that one wonders where to place him. He was, apparently, content to be regarded as a skilled craftsman. There was no need to have any artistic pretensions when fame could be secured by diligence and by having a shrewd idea of what would appeal to the public. It may be that he achieved success by telling people what *they* wanted to hear instead of saying what *he* felt. Barrie was more like a freelance journalist, tailoring his material to suit the market, than an artist prepared to risk unpopularity. Realising that there was money to be made from stories about humble Scottish life, he devoted all his energies to that task. When it became clear to him that the theatre offered greater scope for his talents—especially his ability to write vivacious dialogue—he plunged into the second phase of his career. It would seem that he was more anxious to gain immediate recognition than to write something of enduring quality. There was enough satisfaction to be had from rising from obscurity without seeking the approbation of future generations. In *Margaret Ogilvy*, however, he wrote one passage which suggests that he was anxious to make a lasting mark. He confessed to having been deeply impressed by these lines of Abraham Cowley:

> "What shall I do to be for ever known
>
> And make the age to come my own?"

The only play which gives any indication of having been written with a glance towards posterity is *The Boy David*. In it, he made few concessions to popular taste but cynics would say that was simply because he was out of touch with the theatre-going public by that time. On the other hand, some admirers of that work have suggested that it stands in relation to Barrie's other plays as *St Joan* does to the rest of Shaw's. It was Barrie's only attempt to grapple with the mysteries of Eternity—as opposed to Never Never Land.

If Barrie wished to be remembered, above all, as the author of *The Boy David*, it has not worked out that way. *Peter Pan* has brought him much greater renown but its prolonged popularity may have done more harm than good to his reputation. It has probably magnified the view that he was obsessed with motherhood, and it has left the impression that childish whimsy was his strongest suit. Writing entertainment for children was a digression rather than a central part of his work.

His ability to strike a balance between comedy and pathos set him on the road to success. *Auld Licht Idylls*, *A Window in Thrums* and *The Little Minister* might have been insufferable if he had kept his sense of humour in check. Sentimentality was beginning to get the upper hand in the two books about Tommy Sandys.

Around the turn of the century, when he wrote the novel *Tommy and Grizel* and the play *The Wedding Guest*, Barrie was in danger of becoming very solemn and ponderously concerned with the plight of women exploited by unscrupulous men. He was incapable of conveying the tensions of physical passion, and pity seemed to turn to pulp in his hands. The romantic charm of *Quality Street* was much more popular than his attempts to deal with emotional problems and sexual conflicts. Comedy had re-asserted itself and there was none of the old purple poignancy in *The Admirable Crichton*, *What Every Woman Know*, and *The Twelve Pound Look*. In these three plays, he touched lightly on social questions and left his audience with something more substantial to think about than the future happiness of Phoebe Throssel. He had the audacity, at the beginning of the Edwardian era, to suggest that the ruling classes were incompetent and that a born leader could not expect recognition. He shirked the final issue of *The Admirable Crichton*, however, by making Crichton cringe. Shaw would have given this character a formidable farewell speech that would have left Lady Mary and the audience in no doubt as to what was "wrong with England." Barrie also took the easy way out of *What Every Woman Knows* by showing that Maggie was quite happy to be her husband's servant rather than his equal partner. She, who has every right to call the tune, meekly inquires: "Am I to go? or are you to keep me on?"

Only in *The Twelve Pound Look* did he stick to his guns. Sir Harry Sims suffers from even greater delusions of self-sufficiency than John Shand, but no little woman snuggles up to him at the end and begs for reconciliation.

For once, Barrie had been able to carry a play to its logical conclusion instead of wrapping things up so that everyone lived happily ever afterwards. For Sir Harry and his kind, time was running out, and women were no longer dependent on them. Though it was a very light-hearted assault on the overbearing smugness of the "master of the house," it was one of the sharpest and most skilfully constructed of Barrie's plays.

Instead of continuing to write comedies with a satirical edge to them, Barrie wandered off into realms of fantasy. Excursions into Lob's Wood or "The Island That Likes to be Visited" were the things which distinguished him from other dramatists. Maugham and Galsworthy could compete with him on a mundane level but they were no match for Barrie when he invoked supernatural powers and gave his characters a second chance in life or whisked them away into the empyrean. Sentimentality came surging back to spoil two of the most substantial plays of his maturity—*Dear Brutus* and *Mary Rose*. In the latter he expressed the conviction that "Happiness keeps breaking through"—a comforting thought which formed the underlying theme of nearly all his work. Adversity, old age and death were too unpleasant to be contemplated. They were put to flight by Peter Pan's battle-cry: "I'm youth, I'm joy, I'm a little bird that has broken out of the egg."

The dry, wizened little man, bowed down with honours and well-acquainted with grief, was infatuated with Youth. As James Agate said of him: "To keep young is the great adventure." A fair proportion of J. M. Barrie's work lived up to that, even if this hard-hearted age has barred the windows through which his fancy often took him.

93

THE PLAYS OF J. M. BARRIE
(with dates of first London productions)

1891 Becky Sharp
      Ibsen's Ghost
      Richard Savage (in collaboration with R. B.
        Marriott Watson)
1892 Walker, London
1893 Jane Annie (in collaboration with Arthur Conan
        Doyle)
1894 The Professor's Love Story
1897 The Little Minister
1900 The Wedding Guest
1902 Quality Street
      The Admirable Crichton
1903 Little Mary
1904 Peter Pan
1905 Pantaloon
      Alice Sit-by-the-Fire
1906 Josephine
      Punch
1908 What Every Woman Knows
1910 Old Friends
      The Twelve Pound Look
      A Slice of Life
1912 Rosalind
1913 The Will
      The Adored One
      Half an Hour
      The Dramatists Get What They Want

1914   Der Tag
1915   The New Word
       Rosy Rapture, Pride of the Beauty Chorus
1916   A Kiss for Cinderella
1917   Seven Women (revised version of "The Adored One")
       The Old Lady Shows Her Medals
       Dear Brutus
1918   A Well Remembered Voice
1920   The Truth About The Russian Dancers
       Mary Rose
1921   Shall We Join The Ladies?
1927   Barbara's Wedding
1936   The Boy David

THE BOOKS OF J. M. BARRIE

Better Dead
Auld Licht Idylls
When a Man's Single
An Edinburgh Eleven
A Window in Thrums
My Lady Nicotine
The Little Minister
Sentimental Tommy
Margaret Ogilvy
Tommy and Grizel
The Little White Bird
Courage
The Greenwood Hat
Farewell Miss Julie Logan

SELECT BIBLIOGRAPHY

J. A. Hammerton: The Books of J. M. Barrie
J. A. Hammerton: The Genius of J. M. Barrie
Denis Mackail: The Story of J. M. B.
W. A. Darlington: J. M. Barrie
J. A. Roy: James Matthew Barrie
Cynthia Asquith: Portrait of Barrie
George Blake: Barrie and the Kailyard School
Allardyce Nicoll: English Drama 1900-1930
James Agate: At Half Past Eight
Janet Dunbar: J. M. Barrie: The Man Behind The Image
H. M. Walbrook: J. M. Barrie and the Theatre
Letters of J. M. Barrie edited by Viola Meynell
Plays and Stories by J. M. Barrie, edited and introduced
    by Roger Lancelyn Green
Plays of J. M. Barrie edited by A. E. Wilson
Ibsen's Ghost edited by Penelope Griffin
Collected Letters of Bernard Shaw, edited by Dan H.
Laurence